All Such Fun

by Michael Pope

The Sporting Life

First published in Great Britain 1992
by THE SPORTING LIFE
Orbit House, 1 New Fetter Lane, London EC4A 1AR

© Michael Pope 1992

ISBN 0 901091 59 6

Printed and bound in Great Britain by
Bath Press Limited, Bath and London

Cover designed by ReproSharp Limited, London EC1N 8UN
&
Printed by Ark Litho Limited, London SW19

Contents

List of Illustrations

The author and publisher are grateful to the following sources for their kind permission to reproduce illustrations:–

Foreword

All Such Fun started life as the first Michael Pope article which appeared in The Sporting Life issue of July 11th, 1991. Nobody, least of all me, and even more so Michael Pope, could have predicted what followed. That 'Pope-opener' created such interest that Michael's further adventures were eagerly awaited by a growing band of followers.

At a time when so many in racing can only cast gloom and doom on the sport, Michael's taste of better times past came as welcome relief. In an industry that seems to take itself all too seriously the Pope misadventures have provided a much needed look on the lighter side of racing life.

It is true that Michael was fortunate in being born into a background of privilege. His owners really were in it for the fun. Monetary matters were an inconsequence.

Yet it is the impish humour of the man that makes it all such fun for all who come into contact with him. His ability to see the funny side of any situation and actively seek it is utterly infectious.

Michael had never written a jot until he began writing his articles for The Sporting Life. He writes as he speaks. A rare talent for such a fluent raconteur. His style is a straight reflection of the man he is.

It very quickly became obvious that we had to put the collection of Michael's stories into a book, if only to satisfy his ever-increasing readership.

When we were mulling over the title across the rims of well-filled wine glasses it needed no mindsearching. "It really was all such fun," said Michael. All Such Fun it is. The first book by Michael Pope, which, I suspect, will go the same way as his articles in The Sporting Life …. on … and on … and on.

Mike Gallemore
Editor
The Sporting Life

Preface

by Michael Pope

How lucky I am to have lived such a happy and exciting life whilst surrounded by a lovely family and many true friends.

Having been blessed with more than my fair share of good fortune in the past I set out to recall a few light-hearted incidents as a form of relief from the present day doom and gloom in racing.

To my surprise the response was so contagious I was encouraged to scribble thirty such stories in twelve months, by which time a wide circle of racing folk were calling for a book.

Mike Gallemore, The Editor of The Sporting Life, kindly offered to undertake the task personally. I only hope those who read the stories gain as much fun as I did compiling them.

Finally a word of thanks to those who agreed to be involved and provided pictures to help enhance the tales. A very special thank you to Pat Mather, my secretary for more years than it would be fair to disclose, and to my artistic niece Ginnie Pope for her cartoonish works of art. Thanks also to Emma Hart and Peter Gomm for producing the book.

The Sorcerer's Apprentice

I N THE autumn of 1968 at the Newmarket Horses in Training Sale I bought a horse called Alvaro for 2,300 gns. He was a very good sort and I fancied him first and foremost as a potential hurdler.

He was knocked down to me for less than I expected, possibly because there were a couple of snags to him - his form on the Flat was very moderate, and a short sinister note in the catalogue stating 'has been seen to crib bite' would not enhance his value.

I bought the horse for Mr Billy Fraser, who later became Lord Strathalmond and Chairman of BP. He was a grand person, very sporting and with the right attitude towards ownership. He viewed racing purely as a sport with no expectations of making it pay.

He once said that rich men either kept a mistress, a racehorse, or both, but personally he preferred to squander his money on horses. One could always put a bullet in the poor beast when it had served its purpose but not so with the other luxury.

Alvaro travelled back to my yard at Streatley from the sales together with another colt I'd purchased on the same day called Sky Rocket for 3,700 gns.

Two boxes had been set fair for them adjacent to my house. I went to bed early after a long, tiring day.

About midnight I was awakened by a most weired noise and, after listening for a while trying to work out what it was, I very soon cottoned on.

It was of course the sound of a horse wind-sucking, and this one was obviously a very chronic case. Although the catalogue had inferred that the horse had been seen to crib bite, it didn't mention that he could awake one out of a deep sleep at 20 yards.

By this time my wife Kay had woken up asking what was wrong. I said: 'I've bought a right stumer today, hark to that flipping colt wind-sucking.'

Jokingly, I said: 'If Billy won't take him I'll give him to you as a Christmas present.'

The next morning the head lad Jack Maunder came down to feed as usual around six o'clock, my cue to get up and get cracking.

While shaving I used to pop my head out of the window and ask if they had eaten up.

'Yes, they've all licked out, but that new bay colt in the corner box, which came in late last night is a bloody cribber.'

I replied in a voice hopefully devoid of surprise, for fear of being considered a prize mug, 'Yes, I know, that's why I got him so cheap.'

Both new horses were only led out that day and as they walked round the yard I liked them even more than I had at the sales, except that Alvaro had a great big belly on him, which of course was inflated by sucking wind.

Mind you I had been warned, after buying them, by certain trainers who love to put their oar in, that Sky Rocket was the biggest dog in Newmarket and Alvaro too slow to catch a cold.

Listening to Alvaro's ghastly addiction on and off through the second night I decided that drastic measures had to be taken. None of the usual old remedies such as grids, straps, bibs or pig shit mixed with vaseline would be man enough to deter this fellow.

The next morning, when belting across from one gallop to another on my hack, trying to watch two lots working at once, I got tangled up in electric wiring used by the farmer to graze his sheep.

Having disentangled the horse and myself I found the shepherd to apologise for the awful mess I had caused, then set off home for breakfast. On the way I suddenly thought 'Hallelujah, I've got it.' Why not put an electric wire round the inside of Alvaro's box? That'll teach the bugger to make me look a bloody fool.

Firstly every protrusion in the box would have to be removed. The manger, water bucket holder, wall rings and rack chain, etc. Then the concrete block walls would have to be plastered to a completely smooth surface, and the blacksmith could make flush grids for the door and windows.

But what's the poor devil going to eat and drink out of? No problem, a very light, plastic washing-up bowl and bucket, both unattached and on the floor.

Now to put the 'Pope patent' into action. I planned to install an electric wire held by small brackets protruding about six inches from the walls at the normal cribbing height and with a rubber handled connector at the doorway.

I explained the scheme to my head lad, who obviously thought I'd gone bonkers. He said: 'The horse will go berserk and kill himself thrashing about.' I replied: 'Be that as it may, if we can't cure him he's better off dead.'

I intended to have a bash come what may and Bill Fraser agreed with me.

Luckily, I had a very good odd-job man called Bill Fiddler, known in the yard as 'old misery guts' because he never smiled. I told him I wanted the job done pronto, and to jolly him on I promised him 50 quid if the horse won a race.

While he got cracking I went off and bought a car battery, the necessary wiring, a transformer and hand connector to complete the circuit. The latter would be fitted on the door post so that the lads could disconnect the circuit, for obvious reasons, before entering the box.

The job was completed in two days and Alvaro was put into the 'chamber of horrors', as the lads called it, at evening stables. Before connecting up, I put the transformer to as low a voltage as possible then stood back to await events.

After walking around snorting with suspicion, he touched the wire with his muzzle, shot back like a mad thing and connected with the wire behind him.

Pandemonium reigned, rearing kicking and sweating, but suddenly he froze in the middle of the box, obviously terrified to move and blowing like a grampus with his eyes popping out of his head like organ stops. The only damage was a bit of skin off his knee and hock, with a bang over his eye.

That night the horse ate up from his plastic bowl on the floor, drank all his water and nibbled most of his hay from a net suspended on a rope from the ceiling. The contrivance worked a charm and I was naturally more than chuffed.

Within a short time he looked an entirely different animal, having lost his great big pot belly, which had quite obviously been causing him a lot of discomfort, and was also stopping him from being able to show his true capabilities.

The only drawback to my invention was that the lads occasionally forgot to break the circuit before entering, and touching the wire let out a scream, coupled with a string of very ripe language.

Alvaro had now started to work really well and I was conjuring up ambitious plans, especially as he was right down at the bottom of the handicap. He appeared to be a tough customer and I could visualise him running up a sequence of wins before the handicapper could clobber him.

I ran him first at Ascot on April 11, 1969, in an amateur riders' race, ridden by Bill O'Gorman. We had a fair punt and collected without any problem. Incidentally, old misery guts copped his 50 quid from me, and a handsome present from Billy Fraser. This did raise a semblance of a smile.

Alvaro's next entry was in an apprentice race at Epsom, 13 days later. He looked a certainty to follow up if I could find a really good boy to steer him, preferably one who had not ridden a winner, and hence was eligible to claim a few extra pounds.

The next day we had runners at two meetings and Kay was going to look after my owner at Newbury. I had an idea Frenchie Nicholson or his wife Di would be there, and if anyone could recommend a likely boy they could, having produced such good jockeys as Paul Cook, Tony Murray and many others.

Kay returned home and told me she had chatted with Frenchie, who had said: 'When Mike hears that I've recommended a 17-year-old boy he's never heard of called Eddery, who has had over 50 rides and never ridden a winner, but in my opinion is the best I've ever handled, and will be champion jockey one day, he'll think I'm sloshed or crackers.'

Frenchie's word was good enough for me, drunk or sober. I rang Di the next day to book the boy for Epsom. She thanked me very much, saying his name was Pat Eddery and he would be at Epsom in plenty of time to walk the full course.

On the day of the race I went to the weighing room and asked to see the lad. He immediately struck me as a bright, intelligent youngster, smartly dressed and very respectful, as indeed were all the Nicholson team.

When he came into the paddock he showed no sign of nerves, was cool, calm and collected and, with a touch of his cap, politely addressed those present as Sir or Madam.

Watching him canter down on a nice long rein, he sat like an old hand, with the style of Joe Mercer, a fact that impressed me sufficiently to double my bet.

In the race he did as he was told and won comfortably. When he returned to the winning enclosure he remained calm and was able to answer my questions without puffing or stuttering as so many inexperienced youngsters do.

Billy Fraser was naturally delighted and said he would like the boy to continue riding the horse if I was agreeable.

The next venture was at Newmarket, just six days later, where he won again, virtually on the bridle. Nine days on, in he went again at Kempton with even more ease.

I'd become so impressed with Pat that I aimed to put him up on some of my other horses and asked if he could come down and ride a bit of work.

Frenchie said he didn't like his lads staying in the trainers' hostels overnight because they might learn bad habits. Kay offered to put Pat up at our own house in a bedroom on the ground floor in which a number of senior jockeys frequently dossed down overnight to ride gallops the next morning.

Two of my own apprentices asked if Pat would like to go to the cinema with them. He said 'yes, he'd like to but didn't have enough money on him, adding that Mr Nicholson purposely kept his apprentices short so that they couldn't go out on the town and get into trouble with birds and booze.'

Judging by the way his youngsters turned out, the strong discipline he inflicted more than paid off.

ONE-TIME crib-biter Alvaro wins at the Epsom Spring meeting (above), a first success for young apprentice Pat Eddery. Sky Rocket, partnered by Eddery (below) wins the Wokingham from Spaniard's Inn and Chris Dwyer on the rails and Bunto, ridden by Peter Madden, extreme left.

Alvaro was in again at Salisbury, only five days after his Kempton win, but as he was eating every oat and as fresh as paint we decided to go to the well yet again, with the same result, a very easy win.

As soon as I got home I went through his immediate engagements very carefully. There was an ideal race at Doncaster on May 23, only eight days later, and provided he remained in good form I planned to run.

I also had Pheidippides entered the same day, an old evergreen now 14 years old, still an entire, and bidding for his 15th win. He was a really classy old horse by Court Martial and, having won the Gimcrack Stakes, he had been retired to stud in Ireland with a full book of mares, only to prove totally infertile.

Nowadays he had his own ideas about racing and needed a very good and sympathetic pilot to kid him to exert himself. I suggested to his owner George Clover that Pat should ride, and he readily agreed.

Bill Fraser booked an aeroplane to fly up to Doncaster and invited Pat to come with us. It was, in fact, the very first time the lad had flown, and to our amazement he slept practically all the way there and back, depicting his ice-cool temperament even at such an early stage of his career.

**PHEIDIPPIDES winning at
Doncaster ridden by Pat Eddery in May 1969**

He rode both horses to perfection, notching up not only his first ever double, but the sixth winner of his career, all within 30 days.

Just to confirm that Pat was something really special, he won the Wokingham for me on Sky Rocket at Royal Ascot on June 20. When I congratulated him on having ridden a very good race, characteristically he wouldn't take the credit, saying: 'It was thanks to the horse drawn in the next stall to me, he got very upset and crashed about, making a terrible rattle, which terrified my fellow, who shot out of the stalls and went like hell out of the night.'

Before Pat's first success he told me he was seriously considering giving up racing as he felt he was not making the grade as a jockey.

Now he is one of the greatest, if not the greatest jockey in the world. He is also just as nice a fellow as he was the day we cheered him home at Epsom on his very first winner more than 20 years ago.

ALVARO and Pat Eddery
being congratulated by Di Nicholson.

A Beauty That Was Skin Deep

I HAD the good fortune to train a sweet old horse called Teddy Tail, a very ugly black gelding with a ewe neck, hocks in the next county and unbelievably long pasterns.

In spite of being a ravenous trougher he carried precious little flesh, and although far from a thing of beauty, was very sound with the heart of a lion and totally genuine.

Provided conditions were to his liking he could be relied upon to give his best whenever required to do so.

In those days I fancied trainers made more definite plans for their horses, scheming and planning with precision towards a selected contest. Nowadays it seems rather a hit-and-miss affair, if you win it's great, but if you don't it's a pity.

Maybe the new entry system has something to do with this day-to-day attitude. Also the bush telegraph is much more accurate. Whatever the reason, it certainly seems much harder to organise a little touch without the world and his wife knowing all about it.

The race we set our sights on for Teddy Tail was a selling hurdle at Warwick early in 1954 and the more rain that fell the better his chances as he revelled in hock-deep going.

Warwick was possibly my luckiest and certainly one of my happiest hunting grounds, but I knew I would be accosted as soon as I set foot on the track by a host of punting friends including three very sporting farmer pals who all owned horses with me and were born gamblers ever ready for a hefty wager on horses or turn of the card.

I wouldn't normally leave them out, but on this occasion I planned to employ the guessing game.

At that time Dick Hern was my assistant and I hatched a scheme that he should clap the tack on the old horse as early as possible - made easier by the fact that the race was the first on the card - then make himself scarce until the last moment before belting off to the paddock just in time to give the jockey a leg up.

Incidentally, Derek Weeden was the pilot and had deliberately not been given any orders, although I suspect he sensed there was something afoot.

Together with Tim and Alec, my mother and father, I parked in the area reserved for horseboxes, well away from the Owners and Trainers for obvious reasons.

Meanwhile Dick, having saddled up, darted to the Gents adjacent to the weighing room. He had reconnoitered this as a likely place to hole up, being within earshot of the loudspeaker ordering jockeys to mount.

He locked himself in and settled down on the seat to await the signal for action. The delay seemed eternal, while the atmosphere was far from savoury, and the only reading material available was an incomplete railway ABC, pages of which had obviously been extracted for purposes other than travel information. Nevertheless Dick swears to this day he can tell you details of trains from Warwick to Birmingham and back.

Eventually the moment arrived for jockeys to mount. Out shot Dick just in time to say to Weeden, as he eased him into the plate: 'The Guv'nor says to jump him off, make all, and don't win too far.'

By this time the skies had opened and the rain was tipping down much to the delight of the party hiding amongst the horse boxes who by now had decided it safe to venture from the car and make for the course.

They arrived just in time to scramble up on to the Trainers' stand to hear the announcer say: 'They're off and Teddy Tail goes straight to the front'. Jumping like a buck he increased his lead and, thoroughly enjoying the bottomless ground, won by three-quarters of a length hard held.

Weedon had carried out his instructions to the letter.

While this phase of the exercise had gone according to plan, a hefty wager which included bets for all the farmer chums, had been executed by probably the shrewdest SP operator in the business.

They say he employed a team of runners up and down the country placing fivers, tenners and scores in numerous 'clock bags' at the large factories. As these bags were locked and not opened until after the time of the race not a penny got back to the course or to the bookmakers' offices.

All perfectly legal and adding an air of skulduggery and excitement to the operation.

The code for transmitting such a wager always caused my family much amusement.

The name of a fruit had been allotted to each horse in the yard, and also denoted the amount and nature of the bet. For instance a phone call from my office merely stating 'Two plums for a raspberry, and one peach for an apple' would bring forth hoots of laughter and much speculation as to the horse and size of the bet involved.

Back at Warwick the loudspeaker blurted out 7/1 the winner, when all concerned would have been more than content with 7/2 let alone 7/1. It transpired later that the opening show in the ring had been as low as 2/1 clearly indicating the deception had worked like a charm.

The saga was not yet over. Being a selling race the winner had to be offered for sale before the celebrations could begin. The fact that Teddy Tail was tubed, and adorned with a 'charge' on his near fore to resemble a bowed tendon gave the poor old auctioneer little or no chance of raising a bid.

A disgruntled announcement 'no bid, take him away', met with cheers from the Pope entourage and a wild dash for the bar where champagne corks were popping three races later.

Rumour has it that two of the farmer boys cast up at their homes in the St Neot's area sometime the following afternoon, having taken a route via London and Ladbrokes Club in Hill Street. The third got separated from his friends and ended up in Soho where a kind lady put him up for the night!

During all the excitement at the races, my wife Kay was in hospital with baby at the ready. We had agreed that should the old horse be successful and the infant a boy he would be christened Edward, sounding less frivolous than Teddy. For the record that baby has had two wives, is 34-years old and never answers to anything other than Teddy.

There is rather an amusing sequel to that memorable day. The next time I went to Warwick, a fellow, whom I thought I vaguely recognised, came up to me and said: 'Am I wrong in thinking that the previous time I offered your horse for sale he had a charge on his off-fore leg. I suggest you should be consistent.'

Without considering any possible reprisals in the future I snapped back, 'and I suggest you should mind your own bloody business'.

A few weeks later the old horse was under the hammer yet again after winning another seller at Stratford. Sudden panic that it might be the same auctioneer, but all was well and in any case there were charges on both fore legs this time just for good measure.

**TEDDY TAIL and
Derek Weeden, heroes of the Warwick coup**

While the auctioneer was feverishly trying to get an opening bid, a shrewd old trainer who trained at Royston and had a very squeaky voice, sidled up to me and said: 'I wish I had the guts to bid for that old bugger because I don't believe there is anything wrong with his legs or his wind for that matter'.

Calling his bluff I replied: 'There is only one way to find out, Willie'. I was fairly sure he had his tongue in his cheek because he was a decent fellow and in those days it was just not done for trainers to bid for each other's horses. God help them if they did!

I still chuckle to myself when I think of the operation involving the appliance of the charges. A solid stick of red rubber-like solution, similar to a bar of seaside rock, had to be heated into liquid form before being smeared on to the leg or wherever, but it cooled very rapidly making it essential to be well prepared for action.

While Dick was heating up the potion in a saucepan on his kitchen stove I would be in readiness armed with cotton wool and wooden spoon.

I might add that this operation took place in the solitude of the afternoon when the lads were either in their scratchers sleeping off a skinful of beer at lunchtime, gambling, or hedge-rowing with Muck-sack Millie the local tart.

When the substance was good and ready, Dick held the pot handy for me to dip into with the spoon and smear the first coat onto the tendon, joint, hock or whichever area had been selected for adornment.

Thin slithers of cotton wool would then be pressed onto the sticky substance, followed by further coats of charge and more cotton wool until the required bowed tendon, curb, or enlarged joint had been moulded and shaped to the required state of deception.

There was no way the charge could be removed and would remain in place until gradually peeling off with the hair when shed at the normal time of the year.

I should add that this operation was totally painless, and in no way detrimental to the poor beast, but merely designed to leave his soundness in as much doubt as possible.

It is many moons since I performed my specialised skill as a sculptor of horse ailments and I don't imagine my partner in crime, with a full string of classy horses, has since had need to resort to such skulduggery. However, we had a lot of fun and the object of our exercise was not in vain.

I recall another incident involving the old horse. Having been unplaced quite a few times he dropped sharply in the handicap putting him on a very handy mark which augured well for another stab at the book.

In the very likely event of success I feared I might be asked by the stewards to explain the reasons for discrepancy in running.

The possibilities I mulled over were rather weak and unlikely to be readily accepted unless the stewards were too full of port or too old to care.

Suddenly I had an idea - fit blinkers. He had never had them on before - being so genuine there was no need for them - but this would be a water-tight explanation for the improved form. Even if the brighter officials had their suspicions they could not prove a thing.

All went well and Teddy Tail, adorned with blinkers, won yet again with no questions asked. However, a certain gentleman, universally disliked by the training fraternity, hobbled up to me and said in a most unfriendly manner: 'Pope, you were bloody lucky to get away with that, I suggest you take my advice and keep your nose clean else you'll find yourself in hot water'.

"PARTNERS IN CRIME" ..
Pope leads in his assistant Dick
Hern after winning a race in Italy after the war.

I always suspected by the manner in which he moved, that he had a false leg, which really premised my reply. 'I suggest you stick your wooden leg up your backside'.

This encounter reminded me of a story I had been told in the past, although I cannot vouch if it's true. The same high-ranking military gentleman, who had probably achieved such distinction for long service in either REME or the NAAFI, addressed Capt Neville Crump, a very well respected and likeable character, as 'Crump'.

A highly cryptic reply flashed back: 'You can call me 'Captain Crump', you can call me 'Neville', but you can't flipping well call me 'Crump'.'

Those acquainted with the gallant Captain will guess the adjective he used was not actually 'flipping'.

On reflection I felt maybe I had been a bit unfair to make the crack about his disability, and when he appeared to be missing from the racecourse for sometime I enquired as to his whereabouts, only to be told that he had fallen off his perch.

God rest his soul, I do hope his death was in no way caused by septicemia due to splinters up his blow hole!

It Was All Such Fun

F OR OVER a quarter of a century I had the greatest fun training for Edwin McAlpine, both on the Flat and over obstacles, while managing his stud activities at the same time.

On retirement from the training scene I took over as racing manager and general adviser for a further 15 years. I doubt very much if any two associates ever got as much fun and pleasure out of racing as we did.

Edwin was a delightful person, and a very loyal friend with a wonderful sense of humour.

As an owner he was the ultimate - racing purely for sport and sharing the same enthusiasm for a seller at Ally Pally as for a Pattern race at Ascot. A magnanimous winner and a gracious loser.

Edwin was, and I still am, totally against excessive use of the whip. Supported by him I tried to campaign via the media against the callous practice, however my efforts clearly had little or no effect, as whip abuse is still with us, especially under NH rules and unlikely to disappear completely until owners and trainers unite and make a determined stand. Together they could solve the problem in no time.

Even more important, if they really do care for the welfare of their horses, they must fight tooth and nail against the renewal of live export for slaughter before it is too late.

Edwin and his wife Mollie had a lot of fun naming their yearlings, often without much regard for the sire and dam. His first home-bred he called All Such Fun which described his attitude towards racing and indeed life in general.

Early one morning he phoned me to ask if any of his yearlings were still unnamed and when told that there were just two, a colt and a filly, he seemed well chuffed.

One night he awoke Mollie in the early hours of the morning asking her to grab a pencil and jot down the gist of a dream he had just experienced.

It appears he dreamt that he was in the dark and antiquated old bar on Manchester racecourse when a very large blonde vision, not in the first flush of youth, and with enormous bosoms, flung her arms around him bawling in a dark brown voice, 'Edwin my darling how lovely to see you again after all these years, surely you remember me, I am Aramantha Mavis Hilton Brown.' The exertions of trying to disentangle himself from the lady's cleavage woke him with a start.

No prizes for guessing that the colt was christened Hilton Brown and the filly Aramantha Mavis. The former was very useful and won many decent races, the filly, although only ordinary, did win a contest or two.

A few days before Edwin died he asked me if I thought all the numerous changes introduced by the powers that be in recent times had really improved racing to any great extent.

In his opinion much of the fun had disappeared out of racing - people were inclined to take it all too seriously. Owning horses in the past was a sport for those who could afford to indulge in an expensive hobby, and any prize money was an unexpected bonus.

There is a continuous hue and cry for increased prize money and when it does become available to boost selected races frequently only a handful of runners take part.

Over the years I have heard the Windsor and other executives criticised for poor prize money, even so they always get a stack of runners providing competitive racing, which the public wants.

When they do put up a decent stake more often than not the field dries up to a farcical non-event. If more money is forthcoming from bookmakers or some other source, surely it must be spread across the very bottom end of the market for the benefit of all involved in that sector.

Just occasionally Edwin made such sweeping statements, but on reflection they were seldom without wisdom. We all know that times have changed, but this spontaneous opinion, which emerged through a cloud of cigar smoke, was probably no exception.

With such zest for enjoying life to the full many hilarious and memorable days at the races were inevitable. On one occasion I alerted Edwin that he had two animals due to run a few days hence - Parading in the seller, and Belle Tower in the handicap, both trained by Ron Smyth, still one of the shrewdest in the business and to be ridden by Simon Whitworth a top claiming boy at the time and still a very useful coachman.

These fillies, together with two or three others, Edwin owned in partnership with our great chums Guy and Di Smith - a very long lasting, amicable and successful association. The Smiths raced, and still do, for the hell of it and are always game for a laugh.

Edwin immediately requested his secretary to lay on a helicopter and assure the usual supply of 'medical comforts' in case of turbulence. Mrs Thomas had no doubts at all that this referred to whisky for the boss and champagne for me!

We took off from Dobsons Stud at Henley in a hired machine with a strange pilot as the McAlpine team were all in use. I usually travelled upsides in front with the pilot in case he was unfamiliar with our destination and required guidance as to where and when to land in order to avoid any interference to man or beast.

We were barely airborne when the pilot, not wearing the customary immaculate uniform, in fact looking distinctly scruffy and in need of a short back and sides, lit up a cigarette.

Edwin immediately tapped me on the shoulder and said: 'Tell him to put that thing out.' This I did and a stony silence prevailed for the rest of the journey.

On approaching the racecourse I plucked up courage to ask if he knew where to land and gleaned from a somewhat reluctant reply that the Clerk of the Course's office had assured him the groundsman would put out an 'H' marker.

In the past we flew by fixed-wing aircraft to a nearby airfield and on by taxi. I always had a giggle when landing at Lydd because my old man was stationed nearby in the 1918 war and when asked what it was like, he said: 'Ghastly - nothing but sheep, shit and shingles!'

To my horror I suddenly spotted the marker on the ground clearly much too close to some cars with picknickers enjoying their lunch on the grass behind their vehicles.

Obviously someone had made a real cock-up and I shouted at the pilot: 'You can't land there. You'll blast those poor buggers off the racecourse.'

However he either didn't hear, or didn't want to, and continued to descend.

Within 30 feet of the ground it was clear to see a catastrophe was imminent. Tablecloths, straw hats, plastic mugs, newspapers, you name it, were billowing into the air amidst clouds of grass cuttings.

The horror, disgust and confusion on the faces of the helpless devils was not a pretty sight. One poor lady was frantically grappling with her skirt which was ballooning over her head revealing the fact that she had either dispensed with her knickers in view of the crutchy weather, or they had been blown off! Unfortunately choppers have to cool their engines before switching off and this caused us prolonged embarrassment.

I looked at Edwin who was calmly puffing his cigar and said: 'Maybe I should get out and try to pacify the peasants who are clearly hostile.'

Taking a good gulp of his whisky, he said: 'Good old Pope, you hop out and apologise on my behalf while I finish my drink'.

I jumped down, foolishly expecting the pilot to follow and assist me to calm the situation. A dishevelled group approaching looked extremely unfriendly - who could blame them?

Before I could open my mouth, an aggressive military-looking geezer with a mahogony face, large tash and grass in his hair, yelled at me in a raucous voice: 'What the bloody hell do you think you idiots are doing, you've ruined our day out - Fifi is terrified and has pissed off, I doubt she'll return."

The thought flashed through my mind, could that be his wife or his bit of crumpet!

A tough, hairy, horsey lady was advancing menacingly and by her gait she either suffered powerful haemorrhoids or should have stuck to a side-saddle. Angrily she took up the cry: 'We'll sue you snooty buggers for the chaos you've caused and report you to the Jockey Club.'

I didn't let on that a member of that illustrious body was lying dogo in the back of the chopper!

When I did get a word in I explained that the plane belonged to Lord McAlpine, hoping that a bit of name-dropping might help, but I was silenced very abruptly by the horsey lady who said: 'We don't give a fart if it belongs to the President of the United States.'

Desperately pointing to the 'H' protruding from under the aircraft, I eventually got them to understand that the pilot had in fact landed as instructed, nevertheless we were extremely sorry and would a couple of decent winners earn us a pardon?

The mood changed noticeably, and I suggested that both our runners, Parading and Belle Tower had good chances.

Edwin and the little prat of a pilot were now alighting, so I signalled them to scarper in the opposite direction towards the enclosure

"HAPPY DAYS" . . Michael Pope, Edwin McAlpine,
Guy Smith and Di Smith greet their winner Party Game.

entrance in case their sudden appearance might jeopardise the temporary cessation of hostilities.

I caught them up in the paddock area where our first runner was being saddled. 'Everything all right Pope old boy?' says Edwin.

'I think so,' I replied, 'but I'll tell you something, if these two get stuffed I'm going to leg it across the fields and go home by train.'

With a broad grin Edwin replied: 'And I'll tell you something, I shall be right behind you.'

Thank God both fillies obliged and full of good cheer and Dutch courage we returned to the helicopter. The hitherto angry throng had mellowed, in fact they were positively human offering us tea and cake or a glass of giggle juice.

I asked the military gent, who was clutching a black poodle bitch under his arm, if 'Fifi' was all right. 'Yes', he replied, 'I found her cringeing in the shed behind the number board!'

On the journey home we laughed until the tears rolled down our faces. A couple of winners and full of spirit, combined with the fact that we had for a change made the turf accountants cough a bit, converted the sad plight of the poor picknickers into a great joke which was becoming even funnier with the telling.

On arriving back home Mollie was on the lawn to greet us. 'Well done darling, did you have a bet?' A slight pause before Edwin replied: 'Yes, I had a hundred for myself and a tenner for you on both of them.'

I smiled to myself because he had asked me to put him a monkey on each, and I'd seen him darting to the ring just before the off - which usually indicated a top-up!

An In-And-Out Performer

A NY TRAINER will tell you that his first winner is something really very special and I shall certainly never forget mine. A horse called Coup De Myth gave me that thrill in 1947.

I'd been training only a short while, was desperate for horses and delighted when my old man phoned from Sandown Park to say he had acquired another one for me and would I send the box with a lad to pick it up.

When I asked how he had come by this nag he said: 'I'm not too sure you will be best pleased with me.' It transpired he had a good punt on a horse called Coup De Myth which was 11/8 favourite for the selling hurdle and in his opinion had been a very unlucky loser so he decided to claim him.

While he had heard me say 'Woe betide any trainer who bids for another trainer's horse,' he wasn't sure whether such a gentleman's agreement applied outside the trade. He had no idea how to go about doing the dirty deed so kidded a pushy old girlfriend, who was game for anything, to do the job.

When the trainer heard that he had lost his horse he went berserk and called my old man everything he could lay his tongue to. A follow-up request for the lad to make the horse comfortable and leave a rug on him until arrangements had been made for his collection really stirred the pot!

While all this was taking place I was frantically thumbing through the form book to see if the horse had any form. To my amazement he was classically bred by Coup De Lyon out of Diomyth by Diophon and, believe it or not, had been placed second in both the Irish Derby and Guineas only the season before, yet unbelieveably here he was as a four-year-old in a selling handicap hurdle with a mere 10st 5lb on his back.

However, my enthusiasm waned somewhat when I spotted the letter 't' against his name indicating that he was tubed. Two of my small string already had holes in their necks, the noise on the downs in future would be deafening and I was the sole 'tube cleaner' because the lads said it made them puke.

When the box pulled into the yard I rushed out to see what sort of screw had cast up. To my surprise there stood a really good-looking copper chesnut full of quality and obviously a high class colt who had seen much better days. Incidentally he had a rug on and had been dressed over.

A few days later I got our vet, the late Percy Male, to examine the horse and advise us about his wind. A Hobday operation was recommended and duly performed, while the hole in his neck was stitched at the same time.

After a short spell of light work I started to canter him and, to my delight, he appeared to be clean of his wind, at least in third gear. He went from strength to strength and when the weights for a selling handicap hurdle at Southwell came out I thought he can win that with one leg tied up.

A bit cocky I suppose for a trainer as yet not blessed with a winner, but I had had a good feel for the game having helped to prepare, together with Dick Hern and my brother Barry, a lot of winners in Italy and Austria while awaiting repatriation after the last War.

The nearer we got to Southwell the more confident I became since the going was sure to be in our favour.

My wife, Kay, and Barry had been given the task of executing the family commission. Armed with fistfuls of cash they rushed up and down the lines of bookmakers taking the best prices available while I was clapping the tack on.

We met up on the stands and the atmosphere was clearly tense. I could hardly hold my glasses steady during the race, but the old horse pinged every hurdle and won comfortably by four lengths.

During the race, Kay agitated and smoking like a chimney, got her cigarette tangled with a lady's hat which was draped with veiling and it immediately caught fire!

Leaping off the stands shouting apologies, we almost ran into the unsaddling enclosure.

'Never in doubt, he won with a nice bit in hand and is a lot better than a plater,' said Tony Mullins, the jockey.

Our great friend Frank Cundell while offering his congratulations said: 'Mike, you see those two spivvy looking blokes over there, I've just heard them say they're going to buy your horse. Get someone to bid for you, pretend you're not interested, and I'll deal with those spivs.'

At that moment Di Walwyn passed by and I asked her if she would bid for me. She was a great sport and immediately agreed.

The spivs were bidding furiously, and I feared we would lose our first winner but suddenly they dropped out.

Looking across, I saw Frank talking to them in a confidential manner, whereupon they shook their heads and walked off. Di gave one more nod and the hammer fell at 240 guineas.

Off we went to the bar with Di and Frank for a few jars of bubbly. When asked how he worked the oracle, Frank said with a wiry smile: 'I told them the horse was a cripple and would be as lame as a cat in the morning. They thanked me for marking their card!'

And now to collect the filthy lucre from the ring. This in fact took some time as the bets had been spread with numerous bookmakers. The starting price had been announced as 6/1 but the family runners reckoned their average bet would beat the SP.

Having collected the colours from the weighing room, we were about to head for home when the loudspeaker announced: 'Will the owner of car number so and so proceed to the car park with haste as the vehicle is on fire and the doors are locked.'

I turned to Kay and said: 'I really do feel sorry for that poor bugger'. The announcement was repeated two or three times before Kay gasped, 'My God, that's our car.'

We were on such a high with success and champagne not even a burnt out car seemed to matter too much. In fact when we arrived at the car there was thick smoke belching from every orifice of the Pontiac but it was not really on fire and after using a soda syphon to dampen down the smouldering upholstery of the back seat we were able to hit the road.

The fumes were so choking we had to travel with the windows wide open. Who cared? Coup De Myth had won and we were in business.

Not long after, the big 'count' started. Kay and Barry had noted their bets on the back of the bookies' cards. Kay started off: 'I had seven tenners with Happy Harry, eight score with Honest Joe, seven ponies with Big Mac, etc, etc.'

We started to laugh and by the time Barry recalled his bets the tears were pouring down our faces, a mixture of amusement, smoke and alcohol. After numerous recounts we had averaged 15/2, a nice little touch.

The following morning Coup De Myth's legs were as cool as a cucumber. He had licked out his mash and didn't look as though he had been out of his box.

What next, thought I? He was in an open handicap on the Flat at Bath a week hence with an attractive weight and of course with no penalty for the hurdles race.

This looked a heaven sent opportunity to roll up some of the Southwell gains.

Off we went to Bath and on arrival I bumped into Ginger Dennistoun who said: 'You've got a bloody nerve bringing that old plug here for a decent handicap on the Flat after getting him back for peanuts out of a selling hurdle at a gaff like Southwell.'

I replied: 'We'll see about that and I suggest you have a few quid on him.'

Coup De Myth duly won very nicely at a fair price. After the 'all right', Ginger poked me in the back and said: 'Well done and thanks. If that old screw goes to stud I've got a super show pony I'd like to send to him.'

Coup De Myth won many more races both on the Flat and over hurdles before it was finally decided we should find him a kind and caring home as a stallion. The old chap had served us well and deserved a happy ending.

I'd heard from Charles Frank, our vet, that a farmer who lived somewhere near Chipping Norton and had a few mares was looking for a horse to stand at his small stud.

I telephoned him and he agreed to give the horse a good home for the rest of his days while covering his own and a few of his friends' mares.

About three months later I had a phone call to say that regrettably the horse was no good. He wouldn't even look at a mare, let alone cover one.

I told the old man the problem and he said: 'In my opinion he's talking a lot of rubbish. Tell them I'll take him back.'

What now, I thought. We can't handle a stallion in our yard and there is no other job for a full horse. However, a girl called Pam Hope ran a livery yard nearby and looked after my horses when sick, sorry or in need of a holiday.

I argued with my old man that it could be a waste of his money, and our time, but he was adamant that the old horse should be given another chance.

Thankfully Pam agreed to co-operate and we decided to gather a few old barren mares, at no charge to their owners, in the hope of getting him going on the theory that 'any old thing goes to learn on'!

Having spread the gospel around the local horsey folk, an offer of two ponies came up, one of which was Ginger Dennistoun's show pony. A lovely little mare, she arrived mad in season, as apparently she was more often than not, which was just the job for our purposes.

Even so old Myth couldn't care less. Now and again he would make a feeble attempt to draw and then decide that a pick of grass was preferable.

Pam knew an experienced old stud groom called Bill Davies from nearly Coombe Park Stud and she kidded him on to join the team for a full-scale operation the following morning.

We planned to tease the old chap for much longer in the hope of getting him really stirred up before the next attempt.

After a tediously long wait with a few pathetic false alarms we were becoming disinterested until suddenly Pam shouted: 'Look up, he's ready'.

The excitement was intense, everyone leapt to their action stations and old Davies yelled: 'Bring him on steady.'

Clumsily the old horse lurched, grunted and reared up, landing awkwardly and sideways across the poor little pony, who nearly collapsed under the strain.

Frantic efforts to correct his direction failed, and obviously deciding the job was over-rated he slid down slowly in a limp condition.

Disappointing of course, but we now knew it was only a matter of time and decided to put him back in his box while we had a mug of Liptons and a drag before attempting the 'moment critique'.

My brother Barry had joined us by now and he had been appointed as 'tail man' because we didn't want anything to upset such a delicate operation.

This time Myth came out of his box in a much more purposeful manner and started to draw almost before the mare appeared. She too was clearly in the mood for love-making, having been teased and disappointed to distraction.

'Take yer time,' calls old Davies and 'don't bring him on till he's good and ready.'

With that there was a massive roar and the old horse lunged forward up on to the mare, urged on by various coarse remarks from the excited handlers.

Thanks to the timely and accurate guidance of the tail man, Myth was now a certainty to score.

Naturally, we were all highly delighted and needed only to attract some bigger and better wives.

I was training a mare called Indian Morn. She was very moderate and I persuaded her owner to let us cover her.

She too suffered nymphomania as the covering chart confirmed, 11 services in eight days. However, she appeared to enjoy it immensely, while being good practice for the old fella.

By now he was a dab hand at the sex game, if anything a bit too keen and a bucket of cold water had to be at the ready to dampen his ardour when a pretty maiden was the target!

A number of assorted mares came and went during the next few weeks. However, a very special mention must be given to an old mare called Nicotine Nellie.

She was a right old cow and belonged to a very sporting farmer called Jim Reed.

He brought his mare over to the stud himself and when all the aids were eventually applied - hobbles, twitch, boots, the lot - she was trussed up like a chicken.

However, once the horse was aboard she gave the impression she could stand as much covering as a wooden leg would take poulticing.

Jim took his mare home there and then saying he didn't want her covered again. Little did any of us think that a single covering would one day conceive the extremely famous and talented hunter chaser Baulking Green, trained so brilliantly and with such tender loving care, by Tim Forster.

**COUP DE MYTH seen winning at Huntingdon
with Michael's brother Barry riding.**

By now Myth had long since joined Ian Muir's stud at Fawley near Wantage where he continued to cover a full book of mares of all sorts and shapes for many seasons to come, including one called What A Din, a nice little grey mare owned by Miss Retallack.

Yet another fairy story - she produced the mighty What A Myth - a cracking chaser who won numerous top-class races, ending up with the coveted Gold Cup at Cheltenham.

He was a great favourite with Ian Muir and his delightful family. They all played their part at the stud and were very sad when the old fellow, at the age of 24, was found dead in his paddock having shown no sign of sickness or sorrow when turned out as usual a few hours earlier.

From the day my old man claimed him at Sandown Park until the day he died, I like to believe that grand old horse enjoyed all the tasks we subjected him to.

He certainly gave us all a lot of sport while providing two trainers with the unforgettable thrill of their initial winner.

**COUP DE MYTH'S son What A Myth and Paul
Kelleway seen winning the 1969 Gold Cup.**

Little Harry's Shocking Tail

WHEN I was training at Blewbury in Berkshire, there was a typical old Irish lad with a very expensive face who was forever dragging on a butt end which had long gone out. He was a great character known to all the racing lads as 'Little Harry'.

More often than not he wore a long riding mack, nearly down to his ankles, come rain or shine.

He worked for Freddie Maxwell, a grand person and a very astute trainer, who had forgotten more than many of his colleagues ever knew.

His stables were just around the corner from mine and, together with Dick Hern, who was assisting me and lived at the yard, we had some great 'gas'.

One day in the New Inn we heard a true story never to be forgotten. Knowing the local geography as well as we did it was easy to conjure up a very vivid picture of the episode which had taken place around dusk the previous evening.

After Maxie had been round stables, and the horses had been let down, the lads were waiting for their horses' feeds to be dished out, when the head lad said to Harry, who was holding his stable rubbers at the ready: 'Forget that colt of yours, I'll feed him myself before I go to bed, so leave the top door open.'

Just as Harry was thinking, to himself, 'what the bloody hell's going on?', Maxie shouts across the yard: 'You're not going out tonight are you Harry?'

'Not if I can help it, I've got a few bottles of stout in and thought I'd try and pick out a winner for tomorrow maybe.'

As he went off to the hostel with the other lads he thought to himself, 'funny, why is the head lad going to feed my fella, and why does the guv'nor want to know if I'm going out? He doesn't usually concern himself with my welfare.'

Harry had his supper and was sitting by the television in his tatty old slippers studying the likely runners in the evening paper for Bath the next day, where his two-year-old was due to run in the seller.

About an hour later Maxie shouts up the stairs: 'Harry, I've got a job for you. Put your wellies on, get down to the yard and clap the tack on your colt; your rubbers mind, not your jodphur boots.'

Of course, Harry couldn't believe what he thought he'd heard, but having disputed the orders twice, he thought he had best humour 'yer man - else he might turn nasty, obviously he's drink taken, off his nut, or both.'

While putting his tack on the colt, Harry thought, 'poor little blighter. He runs tomorrow, hasn't had any grub and now looks like having to pull out again.'

With that, Maxie popped his head over the door and said: 'Pull out Harry.'

As he gave him a leg-up he said: 'Now then my lad I'm going to tie this battery round your waist and then I'll connect it up to the spurs which I'm going to put on your wellies.'

'Spurs, battery, wellies, yer man's gone stark raving mad,' thinks Harry.

Maxie went on: 'Listen now, these are electric spurs, don't yer know, and when you touch the colt's sides he'll shoot forward like hell out of the night, but for God's sake sit like a church mouse and don't move until I tell you to.'

At this stage perhaps I should explain that the colt had a lot of ability, certainly enough to win the seller the next day, but was a leery little so and so and bad at the gate, being liable to whip round and refuse to start.

'Right, Harry,' said Maxie, 'take him up to the cutting until you come to the tape I've stretched across the track and wait for me there.'

The 'cutting' was a very narrow stony track with high banks on either side leading up to the Downs. Harry did as he was told and didn't have long to wait for Maxie to arrive.

'Now then Harry, line him up to the tape and when I say 'go', let your spurs in and hold tight.'

A pause then - 'Are yer ready? Go!'

Stones flew in every direction, and with a crack around the tail from Maxie's long tom, away went the colt like grass through a goose, belting up the track faster than he'd ever been in his life, until over the hill and out of sight.

Poor old Harry, purple in the face, blowing like a grampus and hanging on for dear life, eventually managed to pull up on the far side of the Downs having purposely steered the colt straight at the wings of the starting gate.

He'd had a very hairy ride, dodging on and off the gallops to miss the chains draped across at intervals to deter cowboys from pinching a quick breeze-up.

Thank heavens the proprietor of these gallops, Mrs Helen Johnson Houghton, didn't catch old Harry because he would have copped a frightful striping, plus an earful of choice language fit to make one's hair stand on end. Maxie wouldn't have accepted the responsibility because he, too, was scared stiff of her.

Come to think of it, Dick and I had to give our hacks a kick in the belly on more than one occasion to avoid her wrath, when in error we had abused her sacred gallops.

Don't get me wrong, we all like, respect and admire her immensely, but when riled she really can mark one's card.

Harry, having rapidly baled out, was leading the colt back in the direction of the cutting only to be greeted by a roar from Maxie: 'Where the bloody hell have you been? I told you to pull up before you got to the Downs.'

Still catching his breath Harry replied: 'If you really want to know I've been to flaming Aldworth and back via Compton.'

Maxie replied in an apologetic tone: 'Fair enough Harry, you did well to stay aboard.'

When they got back to the yard it was all but dark and as Harry was taking his tack off, Maxie called: 'Come on in and have a jar - you've earned it.'

While downing a bottle of Haig between the pair of them, Maxie told Harry to say nothing about the escapade, and if the colt won at Bath he'd get a ton from the owner.

Having staggered back up to the hostel, another lad had just got in from the pub: 'Where yer been Harry, on the Downs with a bird?'

Not wanting to let on he replied: 'Yes, I've been on the Downs, but luckily I didn't see any birds,' thinking of one in particular!

Early the next morning Harry made the colt ready and, before boxing up, the head lad said: 'Now you know why I told you not to put his feed in.'

So far so good, but of course the jockey was not allowed to wear electric spurs, so a dummy pair of Latchford spurs were substituted. He'd been fully briefed about the trial the previous evening and was not surprised at the orders given by Maxie.

'Keep an eye on the starter's hand and the moment he pulls the lever let in your Latchfords and win as far as you like.'

Normally it was preferable not to win a seller further than need be if you wanted to buy your animal back.

Everything went according to plan, the colt shot out from under the tapes, made all and trotted up.

Being a seller the winner had to be put up for auction. A big crowd gathered around the rostrum obviously expecting to witness some furious bidding. Two or three trainers, who had been impressed by the manner in which the colt had won, asked Maxie if he wanted him back.

To their surprise he shook his head, saying: 'No thank you, bid if you want him, he's had a nasty shock and may never jump off again.'

I was at the races that day and I just wondered if Maxie was kidding them. But no, he never nodded once and the horse was knocked down to a bloodstock agent from Belgium.

[33]

"LITTLE HARRY" . . . just
electric in the saddle.

Harry copped his hundred quid and went home with bridle, bucket and paddock sheet, but minus the colt. He really loved the horses he looked after, although I doubt he shed many tears over the loss of this one.

That night Harry got paralytic in the New Inn but nobody took offence, being mesmerized by the telling of the episode which had taken place the previous evening. They fell about laughing until closing time, when a couple of lads took old Harry safely back to his scratcher.

Sometime later Maxie moved to Lambourn and Harry came to work for me. On my retirement he moved to Frank Cundell in the neighbouring village of Aston Tirrold. I am told that one evening, when leaving The Boot in great spirirts and at peace with the world, Harry staggered and died.

"FREDDIE AND NORA MAXWELL" . . . novel way of curing slow starters.

A grand old stableman, he had lived only for his horses and, wherever he is now, of which there can be little doubt, I bet the other inmates know the story of his colt's shock treatment by heart. God bless him.

Incidentally, a few months later I checked the racing results in Belgium to see if the colt had done any good. Against his name, on the only three times he ran, the report read, 'whipped round at start, took no part.'

'Alfpenny's Priceless Schemes

BEFORE THE last war we lived in Thremhall Priory in Hertfordshire, close by Hatfield Forest. In a nearby village called Birchanger resided an incredibly smelly but colourful old character known locally as 'Alfpenny.

His cottage, if you could call it that, was a rickety shack deep in the nut woods about the village, sparsely furnished and stinking of ferrets and polecats.

He went past our entrance every evening at a tidy old clip heading for The Nag's Head, and on some pretext or other I often waved him down for a chat, as his tales and yarns were worth a guinea a minute.

He drove a pony and trap - both had seen better days and he referred to the latter as 'me cart'. The pony was called Nobby and was as clever as they come. Just as well, because old 'Alfpenny got so drunk by closing time that Nobby was into his collar and heading for home almost before his boss was aboard.

One day he asked me if I would give him a lift to the boozer as his pony had lost a shoe. At that time my twin brother and I had a very snazzy, albeit rather aged, drop-head MG in which I aimed to give 'Alfpenny a bit of a show.

On pulling up at The Nag's Head near Bishops Stortford after a hairy ride he said: 'You can't 'arf drive a car, sir, I wouldn't be surprised if you could drive a bleedin' donkey.' I never have fathomed the significance of that comparison.

On another occasion I asked him why he wore two pairs of trousers.

'Well, it's like this guv, I've got the backside out of one and the flies out of the other.' Fair reasoning if you come to think of it.

More often than not he used to have a stable bucket full of Cox's Orange Pippins on his cart and in a drunken state would knock on the front door asking my mother if she would like to buy some. Repeatedly, she declined, saying that she had plenty in her own orchard. One day, in a bad mood, skint, and full of ale, he tried yet again, only to get the same reply, to which he grunted: 'They should be as bloomin' good as yours, I got 'em from your bloomin' orchard.'

Some time later I had a lame horse and the vet admitted he couldn't diagnose the cause. I asked 'Alfpenny what he thought.

'It's in his bloomin' foot, you could fry an egg on it.' Having probed around with a rusty old penknife, out squirted a deal of pus. 'There you go, clap on a bran poultice and he'll go level by sparrow fart.'

I remarked that I was surprised the vet hadn't traced the trouble.

'I'm not,' he replied, 'that vet of yours may be all right for constipated pekes, but 'e knows as much about 'osses as my backside knows about snipe shooting.'

Wiping the knife on the seat of his pants, he said: 'By the way, that 'oss has a nasty cracked 'eel which wants a seeing to. Get a jam jar of old maid's water and dab it on three or four times a day.'

I wasn't sure how to come by such a commodity. 'Don't 'ee fret, I'll get 'ee some, there be an old biddy what comes up the boozer, she'll spare us a drop for a large port and lemon.'

Not a very attractive thought, but nevertheless the heel was totally cleared up within a few days.

I thanked old 'Alfpenny with a pint of old and mild for his trouble. He winked and said: 'Old Nell's be real powerful stuff, strong as vinegar and the best in these 'ere parts.'

A few days later, 'Alfpenny came clippety clop into the yard and shouts down from his cart: 'I've heard of an 'oss what'll suit a young gent like you to go 'unting on.'

He was a persuasive old devil and I found myself agreeing to meet him by 5.30am outside The Plough Inn at Birchanger.

When I pulled into the pub yard, there he was sitting up in his cart clearly ready to move off.

'Climb up young man, we don't want to arrive at the Badger brothers' place in your flash car 'cos they'll take yer for a toff and screw yer.'

We eventually arrived at the farm so-called, which in the half light resembled a conglomeration of tumbled down, rusty, corrugated, tin shacks rather than a farm.

'Alfpenny says: 'You keep 'yer whip down and let me do the talking.'

'Anyone about?' A reply comes: 'I be in the barn a milkin, old Tom'll show yer the 'oss. Mind I daresn't see 'un this morn, but I knows I 'eard 'un fart.'

Sure enough we traced Tom down and, grabbing a bridle from the barn door, he starts prattling on about the gelding we were about to view.

'Likely as not the boldest 'oss what ever came out of Ireland, e'd 'ave a cut at Dublin Castle if yer pointed 'im right.'

'Alfpenny stops him short: ' and stand the 'oss on his legs.'

Before us stood a sight for sore eyes. A bright bay gelding with black points, all of sixteen-three, full of quality and without doubt a blood horse. On inspection he had clean limbs with plenty of bone and good feet; he was in fact a horse that would pass the most critical judge.

While cantering round a rough old field, bare as a baby's bum, apart from a decent crop of ragwort and thistles, he took a really good hold and pointed his toe like a racehorse.

I tried to fathom how such a beast had come to be in the clutches of the Badger brothers, and why did we have to view him at such an ungodly hour in the morning.

He'd been freshly clipped, recently shod by a good smithy, mane and tail neatly pulled, and indeed stood out like a sore thumb amidst all the assorted rag and bobtail livestock littered about the place.

I was in no doubt that I must have the horse even if I was forced to beg, borrow or steal to raise the necessary cash.

I nudged 'Alfpenny: 'What will they take for him, and how should I go about doing a deal?'

'Tell 'em he's not the sort of 'oss yer looking for and leave it to me. I'll twist their arm after I've plied 'em with a skinful up the boozer tonight.'

When pulling out for exercise early next morning, up trots old 'Alfpenny with the gelding tied to the back of his cart by a bit of rope.

'He's yours guv for ten score, and I want ten nicker for myself plus the price of the grog I had to pour down their bleeding' necks.'

Without any doubt the gelding had to be worth double that figure. However, I tried not to appear too enthusiastic when saying: 'Fair enough I suppose, it's a deal, but how's he bred, and does he have a name?'

'Alfpenny snaps back at me: 'Don't ask so many bleedin' questions, you've got yerself a cheap 'oss ain't yer?'

Out with the Puckeridge a few months later, my new purchase, now called Merrylegs, had given me a really exciting ride, standing off so far he made me shut my eyes and call a cab at practically every obstacle. I thought to myself 'where the devil has this fellow been, and why hasn't he seen a racecourse?'

I'd jumped down to give him, and myself, a breather as we were both a bit knackered, when up came a farmer fellow I knew quite well, but for the life of me I can't remember his name.

However, I do recall that he had a pretty little daughter called Betty. She could really ride, and as a randy schoolboy I remember watching her perform in point-to-points, the contours of her bum more than filled her racing breeches!

'Young man,' says her father, 'that is some sort of yoke you've got there. Do you know he's the spittin' image of a decent hunter chaser my son won a number of races on for old Charlie Farthingwell before he lost the horse?'

I thought to myself: 'Lost the horse? What's he gabbling on about, does he mean killed, destroyed or stolen?'

At that moment there was a roar from behind: 'Hold up, 'ware a loose one,' and while I scrambled up into the plate a wild-looking beast careered past riderless, scattering us in every direction allowing me to avoid any further questions.

A short while later my aunt, who was only vaguely interested in the horsey scene, said to me: 'Mike, a very good friend of mine with whom I play bridge, and I'm told is a leading light in the Newmarket and Thurlow country, wants to know if you would consider selling your gelding to her.'

I asked how she knew about the horse. 'Well - a farmer who does a bit of dealing and has supplied her husband with hunters from Ireland in the past, saw you out with the Puckeridge recently and was agreeably impressed by the way your fellow performed. Also he was struck by the likeness to one of the best horses he's ever shipped over.'

Incidentally, I had a funny feeling I might be able to guess the answer to the first part of the question I was about to ask.

'What's your friend's name, and has she got plenty of brass, because she'll need it?'

The reply came: 'Lady Farthingwell, and yes, her husband left her a fortune.'

I was naturally very sad to part with the gelding, but in view of the dubious circumstances I thought it wise. The price I asked, and got, helped to ease both my sadness and my conscience. I'd heard tell that the Badger brothers had done a moonlight by now and old 'Alfpenny simply ignored any reference to the horse.

When cubbing the following season, out of the corner of my eye I spotted Mollie Farthingwell cantering across to greet me. I feared I might be in for a grilling, but not so. She was charm itself and, having exchanged a few fineries about Merrylegs, the weather, and her fetching hat, we went our separate ways.

Only a few weeks later I read, via the Press, that the poor lady, together with her sister, had been killed in a plane crash returning from Monte Carlo. Sadly, Mollie had gone to join Charlie upstairs in the graveyard.

To this day I honestly have no idea whether or not Merrylegs was a ringer. However, 58 years on, I doubt if the Disciplinary Committee of the Jockey Club will bother sending an 'agent provocateur' scuttling down into the archives from 15 Cavendish Square.

**MICHAEL POPE and his
bargain buy Merrylegs at the
gates of Thremhall Priory in 1935.**

Fighting Spirit In No Small Measure

IT MUST be 45 years on but I still have vivid memories of one particular day at Windsor races.

I'd trained the winner of the first, a three-year-old seller, with a filly owned by Guy Smith, a great chum since schooldays and normally a most amenable owner.

But on this occasion he needed a lot of convincing to chance running his home-bred filly in a seller - merely to provide a medium for his trainer to bet on.

Like most owner-breeders he was inclined to imagine his geese were swans and this animal was no exception.

However, we both had a reasonable punt and the filly duly won without too much effort, at 9/2 if my memory serves me correctly.

Poor old Guy was ashen white at the thought of losing his filly at the subsequent auction, especially having listened to the jockey's glowing reports. A good jockey, but a terrible judge.

In fact Guy had no need to panic as the trainer of the second had been offered a fair bribe to dissuade him from bidding, and those around the ringside were only there to gawp.

If only a crystal ball had been handy to predict the filly's future she would have received a sailors farewell!

Before moving off to celebrate, George Forbes, the auctioneer, announced that he would be offering a three-year-old called Mon Atout after the third race in which he was due to take part.

In those days it was common practice for horses to be offered for sale in between races, more often than not either useless, unsound or both, and their connections desperate to rid themselves of the beast rather than await the knackerman or the nearest Ascot Sales.

Guy, together with his mucker, plus no doubt the habitual scrounger that hovers around offering congratulations in the hope of 'copping a freemans', spent the next two races drowning themselves in giggle juice.

Eventually wending our way into the daylight I spotted a fine big brown colt with lop ears being led around the sale ring. Clearly it had to be Mon Atout - to whom I took an immediate liking.

I knew absolutely nothing about the horse, but had the strong urge, no doubt inflamed by the booze, to bid for him.

Nodding away as if there were no tomorrow the bidding rapidly soared to one thousand guineas, whereupon the hammer came down with a bang.

I smiled as if delighted, but inside felt decidedly sick, having blown a grand of my own money on him.

Although I sensed that I was the only bidder bar the auctioneer, the fact that there was obviously a reserve made me feel less of a bloody fool.

Herbert Blagrave, the owner, breeder and trainer, put his hand on my shoulder saying: 'I wish you luck with him. He's very sound and has ability, but appears to be faint hearted when the chips are down. Maybe he would be better without his wedding tackle, and with a few hurdles in his sights. If he hadn't reached his reserve, I planned to pick his pockets myself.'

I only had a small yard and all my owners were either relatives or close personal friends, therefore I was loathe to suggest they should take on such a pig in a poke.

Hallelujah! - that evening a smashing lady owner for whom I had trained her very first horse to win a few days previously, flushed by success and a few dry martinis I guess, giggled down the phone: 'I hear, via the bush telegraph, that you got well pissed at Windsor this afternoon and bought a useless yoke that can't go fast enough to keep itself warm.'

'Joking apart, I had a lovely little tickle on your winner and if you're looking for an owner, stick me in.'

The very next morning, I got the vet to relieve the poor devil of his danglers and turned him away to recover from a fate worse than death.

To cut a very long story short we ran him 14 times and on each occasion he jumped so deliberately and carefully he lost ground at every obstacle. We tried blinkers and all known aids without success.

Finally, I recommended his sporting owner to cut her losses as he appeared to be a bogey horse. She agreed and offered to give him to me as a hack.

An old stable lad called Danny, who had spent a lifetime in stables and must have witnessed every trick in the trade, said to me one day: 'I reckon there are races to be won with that new hack of yours. He's a bit of a coward, not a rogue, and he needs a good tonic to give him dutch courage so that he'll have a cut.'

I asked him what sort of tonic he had in mind? 'Oh, a good half bottle of whisky down his neck would do the job.'

My immediate reaction was to dismiss his theory as a load of rubbish, but on reflection, I just pondered whether his advice might be worth a crack.

I would have to administer the tincture personally as it wouldn't be fair to involve an accomplice in such a dodgy exercise, although I can think of one old chum who would have enjoyed the challenge and he doesn't train very far from here. No prizes for guessing his name!

I thumbed through the rule book, together with an old horse doctor and we could not find anything to suggest that the scheme would be frowned upon by the powers that be, although today one would no doubt be warned off for life and thrown into the Tower for such outrageous behaviour.

Having made an entry for a selling hurdle at an obscure little course up the sharp end, the planning and scheming that followed really got the adrenaline flowing.

The more I planned the more I felt the plan worthy of a Nat Gould novel. The operation would have to be performed in the privacy of a loose box as near the time of the race as possible.

In those days, and at this particular track, one could saddle up in the racecourse stables and not necessarily in the stalls provided for that purpose.

When the big day arrived I asked Pat Healy, my travelling head lad, to check the jockey past the scales and bring the saddle over to the stable yard where I would be waiting for him.

Arriving at Mon Atout's box, who should be standing outside but my horsebox driver Bill Wheeler. I told him that Pat would be a while yet and would he please pop down to the weighing room to check that the valet had included a pair of long girths.

As soon as he'd gone I nipped into the box, bolting the door behind me for fear of intruders. The horse was tied up so I took him off the rack chain and brought him round to face the window for more light.

Thinking to myself to play it cool fella and don't panic, I turned the bucket upside-down to stand on, and grabbing the horse's tongue with one hand, took the half bottle of whisky from the window sill with the other.

Sticking the neck of the bottle into the corner of his mouth, I started to drench him. At first he took it surprisingly well, but after a couple of large gulps he choked, smothering me with a mixture of whisky and saliva. Obviously he disliked the taste.

However, I persevered and reckoned I'd got a good three parts down him, which would have to do as time was running out.

So far, so good. But like a bloody idiot, under tension and nervous strain, I'd failed to remove my coat, which was a nearly new camel hair and something rather special, to say nothing of my suede jodphur boots which now looked as if I'd been taken short!

Grabbing a sponge I hurriedly wiped the horse and myself as best I could before putting him back on the rack chain.

At that moment I heard Bill and Pat trying to open the door. Pulling back the bolt, I said: 'Just coming, I was bursting for a pee. You won't need me to help saddle, I'll see you in the paddock.'

On arriving at the entrance to the ring, my old man, in whose name the horse was now running, was waiting for me. Walking in together I said: 'Take a chance and have a few quid on this fellow, I've given him a drop of how's yer father and it might just help.'

Looking puzzled he replied: 'Fair enough, if you say so, but what's that smell? Have you been drinking whisky?'

Before I could explain in comes the jockey wearing the old lime green and purple spots. 'Morning gentlemen, and how will we go today? Phew, what a pong, smells like whisky.'

Changing the subject rapidly, I said: 'Now look here, this lad could have improved quite a bit since you rode him last. Get hold of him, boot him into his hurdles as if they weren't there, and go for the line.'

Turning to the old man I said: 'Put me a ton on will you, I want a quick pee.' In fact all I wanted to do was discard my coat in the cloakroom as I couldn't stand the stench or the embarrassment any longer!

'They're off' - Mon Atout had a couple of lengths lead going to the first where he stood off like a good 'un, landed running and continued to have a right cut at every obstacle.

It began to look as though old Danny knew what he was talking about and the gallop was increasing. Pinging the last he pulled away on the run-in to win by four lengths at 100/8.

On returning to the winner's enclosure, the jockey said: 'You were right guv, he was a different horse today,' and jokingly added: 'What have you been giving him?'

I smiled but made no comment.

That was not the only irregular event in Mon Atout's career. He won a couple more races without any help from the magic potion, making it appear that it had no bearing on the improved form, but I still believe it installed the confidence that he had lacked previously.

The last of his wins was a seller at a small meeting up North, and at the subsequent auction, to my surprise and annoyance, an oldish fellow, who I had seen around the racetracks but could not put a name to, bid me up with such determination, I suddenly thought: 'Right, you old prat, you can have him', and I dropped out.

I wasn't unduly sorry to lose the horse as he'd been a headache along the line. Even so, I had a strong urge to let the new owner know what I thought of him. In those days regular racing folk just did not bid for each other's horses, at least not without prior consultation.

'You miserable old sod, I would have thought you'd know better, just wait 'til you want one of yours back, I'll see you get well goosed.'

An explosion followed: 'Pope, I suggest you apologise immediately and we'll say no more. I am stewarding here today and I am a member of the Jockey Club.'

My attitude changed rapidly and in a grovelling tone I replied: 'I'm very sorry Sir, please accept my apologies, and I do wish you luck with the horse.'

By now, the penny had dropped, he was a fellow who always had a decent chaser or two which prompted me to say: 'He'll never jump fences Sir, I've schooled him but he just can't bend his back sufficiently for the height.'

'Oh, that's no problem, I send all my horses to an excellent nagsman in Ireland for schooling.'

I felt like saying: 'Do you want to bet, both of them will break their bloody necks if they take on the big 'uns?'

However, not wanting to press my luck, I kept my trap firmly shut.

A whisper from above: 'Blow for home' and thank your lucky stars you're still in the business!

For the record, a few months later, while contesting the last of a few abortive attempts at fences, apparently the poor old horse broke his back when falling at the last ditch.

DUTCH COURAGE ... Mon Atout pings the last

**MON ATOUT is led in
by travelling lad Pat Healy**

Bull Cast-off's
Stag-gerring Trial

BACK IN 1961, I was asked by Clive Graham if I would train a horse he would be managing for a decent fellow called Barney Shine, who was entering into ownership for the first time.

I was more than happy to accept as the Daily Express racing columnist was such good company and further involvement with him could only be a bonus.

The animal concerned was Pheidippides, a six-year-old full horse, exceptionally good-looking and bred in the purple by the mighty Court Martial out of Queen Eleanor.

He was owned by Phil Bull when he won the Gimcrack Stakes in 1957 and after two further successes the following season was sold to stand as a stallion in Ireland.

As could be expected, his services were in demand and a list of high-class mares were booked to him. Sadly, he proved entirely infertile and was bought by an owner of Vic Smyth's to go back into training.

After being beaten two necks in the Royal Hunt Cup, he was bought privately on Shine's behalf.

The horse proved to be a perfect gentleman, a pleasure to train and not in the least randy, despite having had a bevy of beauties at his beck and call. He had only one fault: he took a fierce hold and once in top gear it was 'goodnight nurse' for the unfortunate passenger.

During his first season with me he won only one race. It was at Alexandra Park, without any doubt my favourite racecourse. Our jockey that day was Lester Piggott.

I told him to pay heed. 'Take him down at a hack canter, only just out of a trot, with his head tucked well into the nearside rail.'

Barry Mills, the faithful lad who did the horse and really loved him, knew full well what it was like to be carted and normally would not slip the lead rein until the pilot was well prepared for take-off.

However, when Lester said: 'Let him go, he'll be all right,' Barry was reluctant to query the maestro and let the horse go. Away he went like hell out of the night.

Only very old trainers like myself, unless they have already dropped off the perch, will remember this fascinating track, the shape of a frying pan, very sharp bends and nearly all the races starting and finishing immediately in front of the stands.

The runners were supposed to canter down about two furlongs, then hack back to the starting gate. Pheidippides however, was now in orbit, and, slithering round the hairpin bends at a furious rate, arrived at the mile start before Lester could anchor him.

I was already off the stands and away to discuss if we should withdraw. Less composed than usual, Lester said: 'This is a dangerous bugger. He pissed off with me and went round those bends on one wheel. Let him run and if he goes half as fast in the race he'll hack up.'

How right he was. Shooting out from under the tapes, away went Pheidippides at a scorching pace and was never in any real danger of being collared, winning rather cheekily by a head.

On returning to the winner's enclosure, Lester, allowing himself a rare smile, said: 'I reckon I should be paid double fees and danger money for that performance.'

Racing at Ally Pally was something really special and seldom passed without drama - rather like old-time music halls where the audience voiced their opinions in gutteral tones.

The crowd, especially at the evening meetings, were an unlikely blend of Hooray Henrys with bowler hats and brollies, straight from their desks in the City, mingled with rowdy cockneys in flat caps and chokers.

The poor, wretched starter often suffered a verbal barrage of abuse, with remarks such as: 'Don't worry about that one out the back guv, he's not off' or: 'Don't let 'em go yet, old cock, the favourite's not ready.'

The more they heckled him the more frustrated he became - who could blame him?

But it caused some fairly ragged starts, which drew raucous guffaws from the crowd. All good-humoured stuff, adding a bit of flavour to the proceedings.

On one occasion I was on the sharp end of the bovver boys' tongues. There were three runners and a rag in the two-year-old seller; one was trained by George Beeby, one by Frank Cundell and the fancied horse by me.

The three of us were close friends and had travelled to the meeting in the same car. As none of our owners was present we stood chatting together in the parade ring, along with the three jockeys, which I suppose might have given cause for suspicion.

All the jockeys were given the same orders: 'Win if you can, but there's another day if she's not good enough.'

My filly Princess Shumar won by a neck, ridden by Greville Starkey, from George's Wagon Star, the mount of Doug Smith. Frank's was third.

None of us was unduly surprised or concerned by the result, but clearly a section of the crowd were, which was a bit odd as Princess Shumar started at 10/11.

Wagon Star, however, had missed the break, a factor which the commentator didn't ignore, and I suppose this may have given further cause for suspecting chicanery.

However, we didn't wait to find out as we were now under a volley of abuse and scarpered to the weighing room for cover.

Purple of face and short of puff, the starter soon joined us and over a mug of Liptons we discussed our next move. We made a dash for the car park and away down the road to our favourite watering hole for a large nerve restorer.

After Pheidippides had run a few more times, Barney Shine was advised to sell him and look for a high-class yearling with classic potential.

Clive and I were against the idea but were eventually persuaded to enter the old fellow for the Newmarket Autumn Sales.

Watching him walk round the ring as proud as a peacock and looking a million dollars, I felt utterly ashamed to think that I had allowed him to suffer such an indignity. That pang of guilt urged me to take him home, come what may.

I was thrilled to be his new owner for as little as 260 guineas, but relieved when George Clover, a good friend of mine, offered to ease the load and take a half share. I doubt he ever had cause to regret that magnanimous gesture.

Old Pheidippides continued to run regularly from Catterick to Royal Ascot and most venues in between, winning more than his fair share of races when he had the mind to, including three more at Ally Pally, ridden by my own boys Michael Cowley, Jimmy Miller and Fred Messer.

While most of the races he contested those days were either apprentice or selling races, there was little chance of losing him in the latter events, for it would have taken a brave man to bid for the popular old warrior.

However, one day at Windsor a poor, ignorant little creep did have the nerve to give a nod.

Incensed, I shouted to the auctioneer: 'Isn't that gentleman aware that it's not done to bid for this gallant old schoolmaster?'

There was a deathly hush, broken only by the auctioneer. 'No bid, take him away.'

The little man that dared to cock his jaw was totally ignored amidst applause from those around the sale ring.

I venture to add that the rare appearances at the posher meetings, such as Royal Ascot and York, were instigated by George, solely for the purpose of rubbing shoulders with other owners, especially the titled, rich and famous, preferably with vast sporting estates, in the hope of landing large business coups plus perhaps the odd day or two shooting on the grouse moor. He was a crack shot.

By now the old horse was extremely popular with the public. Whenever he won or was placed our mail contained sentimental letters of good wishes from old age pensioners, children and all his faithful fans, enclosing gifts of postal orders for ten bob or a pound to buy a supply of his favourite Polo mints.

There was a likely contest coming up at Newbury, the London Apprentice Handicap, but the conditions stated 'to be ridden by apprentices for their own stables and who have not ridden more than three winners.'

Not having a boy thus qualified at the time, I asked my chum and neighbour Ken Cundell if he had a suitable pilot. Yes, he had - a lad called Barry Hale, but, of course, it meant that Pheidippides would have to join Ken's yard and be officially trained by him.

We used the same gallops and so it was agreed that Hale should climb on board the old fellow and give him a canter, then take him back with Ken's team to Compton.

As usual, he took charge, and, depositing the poor unsuspecting lad at the end of the gallops, headed off home to Wood Farm at Streatley.

However, both horse and jockey were soon reunited and on their way over to Compton. Two days later, Barry rode an excellent race at Newbury and finished second in a large field.

The following season we planned to repeat the exercise, and, prior to arranging his transfer back to Compton, I decided to give him a short, sharp blow-out on his own. This was all he needed in the way of work before the race as he ran best when mad fresh.

No sooner had he jumped off than a large stag bounded out of the wood adjacent to the canter and took up the running.

Pheidippides was having none of that, and, going like the clappers, ranged upsides to finish on terms. An unbelievable sight, especially at sparrow fart when all present were stone-cold sober.

Two days later off we all went to Newbury. That morning Peter O'Sullevan napped Pheidippides in the Daily Express, following his good trial with the stag. Win he did, at 100/7, amidst roars of encouragement from George, Ken, myself and all his faithful fans.

One would have thought he had won the Derby, but all the plotting and scheming involved had been such fun and had now paid off. Isn't that what racing is all about?

One might well imagine that this win would have been a fitting finale. Not so. He continued to enjoy further racing around the country, notching up six more wins and umpteen places while continuing to provide rides for keen young lads desperate for a chance in public.

We were now seriously contemplating retirement as the corns were becoming increasingly crippling.

Adorned with thick felt pads under his plates, off he went to run at Doncaster - his pilot yet another pink-faced youth called Pat Eddery.

Pheidippides duly won and achieved, wait for it, his 15th win at the age of 14 - while still a full horse. Surely that must be one for the Guinness Book of Records?

ABOVE:
Pope lad Jimmy Miller brings home old character Pheidippides from Silver Satellite in a Windsor apprentice handicap in 1967

LEFT: George Clover, part-owner with the author, in his Ascot gear.

Dog's Dinner Brings Me Luck

T HE MORE I see and hear of the training game the more I realise how lucky and privileged I was to have lived and trained at Wood Farm, a delightful old home with a picturesque yard, tucked away from the madding crowd amid the Berkshire Downs.

There were only 19 boxes but to increase the number would have unbalanced the whole scene. Space was at a premium but with a bit of Box-ing and Cox-ing it seemed to work.

Pam Hope, a good friend and an artist at conditioning horses, ran a livery yard nearby and handled those in need of treatment or a rest.

I had a grand team of owners, including my parents, who lived across the yard. The other owners were mainly personal friends prepared to pay for their sport and they treated any financial gain from either prize money or betting as an unexpected but welcome bonus.

Together with home-bred animals, I used to top up each year at the horses-in-training sale at Newmarket, concentrating mainly on horses from the big yards which had to make room for yearlings, especially from trainers who were not too hard on their horses at home or on the racecourse and were prepared to mark one's card while protecting their owners' interests.

In 1964, I was looking for dual purpose animals with enough size and substance to jump hurdles and then hopefully return to the Flat the following season.

Just such a possibility was a three-year-old called Birdbrook, by Mossborough out of Game Bird by Big Game. He was a grey colt, bred by Mrs Jo Bryce at the Moyns Park Stud in the village of Birdbrook.

He had won his maiden but appeared to have let the side down when clearly well fancied on two subsequent occasions.

The horse was trained by Sam Armstrong and it had been my intention to pop down to see him prior to going up to Park Paddocks. He and his wife Maureen were very hospitable, with open house to their friends and colleagues when sales and racing were in town.

However, when travelling down to Newmarket with Frank Cundell, he said: 'Oh, by the way Mike you can scrub Birdbrook off your list; he's wrong off his back. My travelling lad met one of Sam's lads in the club last night and he said: 'Don't touch the horse; he's been lame behind and cooped up in his box for weeks.'

In view of this information, we went straight up to the sales. Standing minding my own business, I suddenly clapped eyes on a fine big grey horse being ridden round the pre-sale ring by a very well turned out stableman with highly polished boots and cloth leggings, riding very deep and sitting as if glued to the plate.

The horse was, of course, Birdbrook and he was jumping and kicking as high as himself.

I thought to myself there can't be a lot wrong with him if he can perform like that. An American agent standing nearby said: 'Say, fella, what a pity that yoke is a screwball. I could have sprung a lot of dough for him.' It appeared the rumour had spread afar.

Even so, I just couldn't take my eyes off the horse and as he was about to enter the sale ring I spotted Sam Armstrong striding across from the car park. As I greeted him he reacted with a smile.

'Hello Mike, what are you doing so far from home, and why haven't you been down to see us?'

I replied: 'I came to try and buy your grey but rumour has it he is unsound.'

In an angry and puzzled tone, he replied: 'What bloody rubbish. It's true he let us down a couple of times when we really fancied him but otherwise he's a damn nice horse.'

Without further ado I decided I would go to eight grand, plus a bit if need be. In fact I got him for 1,800 gns and I'd hardly left the ring before a couple of misery martins couldn't wait to tell me I'd dropped a clanger.

Rather than explain my reasoning, I replied: 'Is that so? Well they say there's one born every minute. Never mind eh, he'll make me a nice hack.'

On the way home I said to Frank: 'Sam would never deliberately put me away. I reckon one or both of those lads were pissed and got their wires crossed.'

He replied: 'Could be. I hope so for your sake.'

On arriving home there was a message awaiting me. 'Mr Armstrong rang to say that if you find anything wrong with Birdbrook you are to return him immediately and your money will be refunded.'

A few days previously a mega rich new owner had given me an order to buy an orange horse for his wife's birthday. No limit was mentioned so I assumed I had carte blanche. I phoned him that evening to say I couldn't find an orange horse but I'd bought a grey for 1,800 gns.

It didn't sound as if he was jumping with joy when he replied: 'The horse sounds too cheap, and in any case my wife specifically asked for an orange animal.'

When I told my wife Kay, she said: 'Maybe the hat episode put him off.'

I'd clean forgotten that he'd been over the previous Sunday wearing a brand new valore trilby and, whilst we were having a drink, Kay whispered to me: 'You know that ghastly titfer. Well your Jack Russell is guarding a nasty-looking chewed mess in the hall.'

Away goes my new owner minus hat! My old man said: 'Looks like you're stuck with the grey horse. Unless you've got another mug in mind I'll be happy to take him.'

I had such a strong feeling about the horse I gave him to Billy Sargison to do, a really good lad and anything he looked after always won races.

After two or three schools over hurdles he proved to be a natural and ready for a very quiet race.

Off we went to Stratford with a good claiming boy called Clive Searle aboard. I told him: 'This fella really jumps but he's not done a lot other than school since I got him, so give him a nice education and let him drop out when he gets tired.'

Get tired? I only wish to goodness he had! Standing off and reaching for every hurdle, he pulled himself to the front a long way out and won by 20 lengths on the bridle at 100/6.

Although we hadn't had a penny on the horse, it at least proved he was genuine, sound and had ability.

As usual my old man took it very well and that evening I had phone calls from a number of jump trainers all wanting to buy, but the response was definite.

'No, I am not interested. Let's have a bit of fun with him.'

He was working so well we decided to cut out hurdling and have a crack at the Flat. He won at Leicester followed by Newbury - when Ron Hutchinson was so impressed he asked to ride whenever free.

By now we had definitely learnt two things. Firstly, he must have the top of the ground, in fact the harder the better. Secondly, he loved to bowl along in front on a turning track.

In the 1966 season, he won five times, followed by three more successes in 1967 and a further four in 1968, all achieved in the same exciting and decisive manner.

The instructions to the pilot were always the same: 'Jump him off, go for the fence and make all, but on no account hit him.'

He had given us all an enormous amount of pleasure plus some very lucrative punts.

One day my old man said to me: 'Before I fall of the perch I'd like to have a grand on a horse just for the hell of it. Up to now a monkey has been my limit.'

Being so genuine and predictable when conditions were favourable, Birdbrook had to be the boy for the job.

He was in at Brighton, where I thought he was a certainty. Everything fell into pattern. Ron Hutchinson could ride, the going was firm, and he was drawn on the fence.

The fact that he had top weight deterred the pundits, but not me as he was such a big and burly devil weight didn't stop him.

I told my old man: 'Bar a fall or a suffragette on the track, this fellow will win.'

I heard him ask Jack Hawkins of Beresford and Smith: 'What price Birdbrook?'

'9/1 to you Mr Pope.'

'Right, I'll have nine monkeys.'

Hardly out of earshot we heard Jack call: '10/1 Birdbrook.'

My old man was clearly insulted that our judgement had been disregarded and shouted back: 'Cheeky bugger. I'll have another monkey.'

**BIRDBROOK, the grey, ridden by his lad
Billy Sargison, leads out the string**

To be fair, Hawkins, a decent fellow but renowned for being tight as a duck's arse, obviously felt guilty. 'You've got 10/1 to £1,000,' he replied.

The grey flyer shot out of the gate and, hugging the rail, bowled along in front to win rather cheekily with the coachman bobbing up and down in his customary manner.

BIRDBROOK lands a
typical all-the-way win.

One more run at Ascot was planned in three weeks' time before he went off to stud. In he went again to complete a highly honourable career on the racecourse, with no fewer than 16 wins without a single crack of the whip, and still as sound as a bell of brass.

As a stallion, he sired many winners, both on the Flat and jumping, from a very moderate bunch of mares.

For example, out of a little selling plater I trained called Wagon Star, he produced Star Bird, a winner of good races including the Challenge Stakes at Newmarket.

He also sired Girl Friend and a very useful filly beaten a whisker in our One Thousand Guineas.

More recently another daughter of his called Best Girl was responsible for Tel Quel, winner of the 1991 Champion Stakes at Newmarket, and the 1992 Aral Pokal in Germany.

I still have one living link with this unique old horse. My 17-year-old hack, given to me many years ago by Edwin McAlpine, is by Birdbrook and, when cantering round a nearby stubble field hanging on for dear life, I kid myself I'm Ron Hutchinson swinging on down the hill at Brighton or into the straight at Kempton.

Hip, hip for those lads that got befuddled with booze, and hooray for the puppy that deterred the intended owner.

**A recent picture of the author
on his hack, a son of Birdbrook.**

**Michael (left) and father
Alec Pope outside Birdbrook's
box in the Wood Farm yard**

A Puntin' We Will Go

I T'S SAD that Birmingham racecourse is no longer operating. It was a very fair track, similar to Newbury and possibly even fairer. Unlike the latter, the draw made little or no difference and in my opinion the fences were the best in the country.

A happy hunting ground it proved for me, both on the Flat and over obstacles, especially as the executive appeared to cater for my sort of horses - plenty of sellers to suit all ages under both rules.

One particular episode I recall with mixed feelings. It was way back in 1954 and involved a little two-year-old filly with a big heart and a big white face called Bienfaisant, by Chanteur II out of Lady Bounty.

She was bred and owned by Miss Gladys Yule, but leased for her racing career to Guy Smith. Guy was, and still is, a very good friend of mine, ever ready for a gamble whether on horses, cards, or a spin of the wheel.

It is said he holds the record for playing poker more hours than any other man - anyway that's what his wife Di reckons!

The filly was starting to show plenty of dash at home and although I hadn't asked her any sort of question I somehow sensed she could be just the article to lay out for an old-fashioned touch if handled with care.

I planned to give her two or three runs to acquaint her with the razzamatazz of the racecourse before subjecting her to a full-scale trial at home.

You might consider that dishonest, but I didn't feel she was physically ready for anything more strenuous at that stage.

The preliminaries over the next few weeks went according to plan with an airing at Windsor and Newbury.

Now for the moment of truth. I had the ideal tackle to tell me the time of day - a two-year-old which had run a close second in a smart seller the week before. It was appropriately called Tenderness, being by Gigantic out of Loved One by Vigorous.

I also had two useful sprinters, Blason and Loll, both of whom had already won decent sprints that season at Hurst Park and Newbury.

I arranged the weights accordingly and decided to have them ridden by my own lads rather than jockeys, as the latter had so many punters in those days the world and his wife would have known the full strength of the trial before I was into my bacon and eggs.

They came five furlongs on the trial ground as fast as they could leg it. Bienfaisant finished upsides the two older horses, with Tenderness four lengths away.

Blason and Loll normally worked about the same speed at home, which confirmed it was a true gallop. I reckoned the form was good enough for any ordinary maiden race but a certainty for a seller.

However, a lot of scheming had to be done before the operation could be geared for action.

First and foremost, I had to get Glad Yule's permission to run in a seller, as the filly was only leased. As she was a wealthy lady who never bet, it was a little difficult for her to understand why we wanted to run in such a contest when the animal was not on the market.

However, she was a good sport and agreed after I explained that it was most important her filly should be made a winner before she eventually retired as a broodmare.

I hadn't the nerve to tell her we aimed to go for a killing but I fancy she'd guessed when she said: 'Fair enough, provided Mr Smith agrees to buy her back whatever the cost.'

SOME PLATER! Bienfaisant
and Joe Mercer run away with the Piccadilly Handicap at Hurst
Park.The previous season she had won at Birmingham in a seller.

GUY SMITH (left), who
leased Bienfaisant from Gladys Yule, and Michael Pope.

Now I had to persuade Guy that my plan was a runner. I told him of the trial, my conversation with Glad Yule and that I was confident the filly would win at Birmingham the following Monday with Tommy Carter at the controls.

At first he sounded decidedly dubious but agreed after I assured him we would be able to buy her back for an absolute maximum of 500 gns.

Mind, I was in his good books because we'd had a fair touch at Worcester only 48 hours before with a horse of his called Mikael III, ridden with great confidence by Johnnie Hislop.

In those days, I had an arrangement with my owners and chums who liked to punt. When backing a horse in a seller I included a bet for them all without their knowledge, and a proportion of their winnings was deducted on a percentage basis towards the owner's cost of buying the winner back.

It also stopped the odd greedy devil from going in early, helping himself and spoiling the odds for the rest of the team.

Nearer the day I phoned Bill Tarrant, a grand fellow well known for operating commissions fairly and successfully. I outlined our plan and gave him a rough idea of the likely total. He replied: 'If you can assure me that none of your team will be nibbling at her in the ring I'll back her on the course as near the off as possible.'

The big day arrived. 'They're off' - and after four furlongs Guy, whose glasses were steamed up and far from steady, said: 'How are we going, I can't see her. Did she get left?'

I replied: 'She's well clear on the stands side with Tommy sitting up like a guardsman trying not to win too far.'

'Oh God, I can't watch,' says Guy, almost as if willing her to be beaten.

She duly won on the bridle by four lengths and after we nipped off the stands I asked Guy to find Bill Tarrant and inquire what price he had got for us, then join me at the sale ring. I had a quick word with the trainer of the second to ensure he didn't rock the boat.

In spite of the auctioneer prattling on about her beautiful breeding and how easily she had won he appeared to be having no luck in raising the minimum bid of 100 gns.

**GORDON RICHARDS on
board Loll, whose work with Bienfaisant convinced Pope
that the filly was a certainty in a seller.**

As a breathless Guy returned to report that Bill had averaged 11/1, suddenly an irate and demented looking George Cooper, the book-maker, yelled at the top of his voice: 'I'll teach you to leave me out you buggers,' and, frantically waving his racecard, shouted: 'One thousand guineas.'

By now poor old Guy looked as though owning a winner was an overrated pastime and mumbled: 'What the bloody hell is the matter with him?'

Hesitating to reply, while giving the auctioneer a quick nod, I told him: 'You know he backed Mikael for us last Saturday at Worcester. Well, I can only imagine he's got the nark because we didn't use him today.'

Two more bids and the filly was ours at 1,150 gns. Both shaken and embarrassed, we were about to head for the bar when Cooper called me to one side: 'I want to apologise. I'm afraid I blew my top because Joe Sunlight had a fair size bet with me and I laid him 20/1 which I stood because I took it for granted you were not buzzing today as you hadn't asked me to do the commission. There was no reason why you should have done. I'm very sorry.'

Joe Sunlight was a fearless mug punter who always backed his own judgement and seldom bet in small amounts.

At a guess I imagine he probably had two or three hundred on Bienfaisant, which would make a nasty hole in any book at those sort of odds.

According to the papers the next day the price we had to pay to retain the filly was a record. However, after we had done our sums there was still a healthy profit and, apart from the unforseeable debacle, the operation had gone entirely according to plan.

Rather bad on the nerves, but a lot of fun with a great feeling of achievement.

Just as well we did buy her back, not only because of the commit-ment to Glad Yule, but the filly went on to win some decent races and eventually as a broodmare she bred many winners, including the more than useful French Parade.

Sadly, Bill Tarrant is no longer with us but when I saw him on his 90th birthday he said with a lovely sparkle in his eye: 'I shall never forget that day at Birmingham. Those were the days, Mike. You certainly kept that one under wraps.'

The One That Got Away

WHILE ENJOYING the recent publication 'Oaksey on Racing' I came across a short chapter headed Blazing Scent. Clearly, the author's reason for devoting space to him was to make the point that the most important qualities in a racehorse are often invisible and that outward appearances can sometimes mean very little.

I had a feeling the name Blazing Scent had a familiar ring to it and as I read on the penny dropped.

In fact, I had personally selected the name for a yearling colt and will record the unorthodox manner in which he was conceived.

One morning some 34 years ago, trainer John Beary phoned to ask if he could send a mare called Frigid Flower to the stallion we were standing at the time, Blason.

He was a good-looking, useful sprinter by Royal Charger out of Sure Shield, by Solenoid, which I trained with a degree of success for Francine Clore, the wife of Charlie Clore.

John said that the mare was in season, that he would like her covered and sent home to avoid the expense of keep charges.

Normally, this practice would be unacceptable both to the stallion and the stud groom. However, John was a good friend and I agreed.

The mare duly arrived - a washy chesnut, light-framed, with precious little bone and very narrow. In fact, she had nothing to recommend her as a broodmare.

My stud groom, a wonderful character and a broad Scot called Frank Horne, was in sole charge of the very small and informal stud.

He ran it single-handed, apart from a snotty nosed village lad with a permanent drip on the end of his nose, and my spasmodic assistance when time from the training side of the operation permitted.

I enquired: 'How many ladies are to be goosed this evening?'

He replied: 'Only the one, but I shall need your help. I teased Mr Beary's mare with the pony this afternoon and she kicked hell out of the trial board. I reckon she's going out and we'll have to rape her.'

He continued: 'Best cover her in the barn. Being a maiden, she'd cart us all over the place out in the covering yard. See you about half-six.'

When I arrived at the barn there was this poor wretched article trussed up like a chicken. One fore-leg was strapped up, a twitch on her nose, another on her ear and hobbles on her pasterns.

I said: 'You're not taking any chances with her, Mr Horne?' He replied: 'No, and I haven't finished yet. I'll blindfold the poor wee lass.'

With that he slipped out of his jacket, put it over her head, and tied the sleeves under her jowl.

I ventured to ask how I could help. Handing me the reins of the bridle and two twitch handles, he said: 'Keep her head tight up against the boards 'cos she's sure to plunge forward when the 'oss gets across her.'

Then off he went to fetch the stallion from his pen.

You could hear Blason coming some way off, shouting and hollering, clearly in the mood for love.

As they entered the barn Horne shouts: 'Hang on man and keep those twitches going.'

With that, Blason bounded on top of the mare and amid screams of unwillingness to lose her virginity the poor beast tried to leap forward to avoid being covered.

On three legs and helpless, she collapsed onto her knees and, knocking me arse over head, I was now wedged against the wall in a sitting position with one of her knees in my crutch.

Horne shouts: 'Come on out from under there, man, the 'oss is nearly done.'

Nearly done, I thought to myself; he's not the only bugger.

With that the horse slid off and somehow I extracted myself from down under and scrambled to my feet.

Having relieved poor Frigid Flower of all the paraphernalia, old Horne said: 'If that mare's in foal I'm Fred Archer.' He continued: 'Just as well the ladies aren't as reluctant as that!'

She was picked up the following morning and returned to Norman Hindes' farm at East Ilsley, where she was a boarder.

I rang Beary to report that his mare had been covered, but I didn't mention the word rape or indeed any of the other sordid details.

A couple of years later my old man said to me: 'I've had a letter from Alice Beary. She is tidying up John's affairs after his death and wants to know if I would be interested in buying a yearling by Blason. She is looking for a good home and a hundred quid.'

I said to Mr Horne: 'You remember that mare we raped in the barn a couple of seasons back? Well, believe it or not, we got her in foal.

Remembering the mare, my immediate reaction was to advise against the purchase, but my old man said: 'I'd like to help Alice, she's a grand person. So be a good fellow, give her this cheque, and do what you will with the yearling.'

When eventually I found the youngster grazing with a lot of cattle and some mares, one of which I thought I recognised as Frigid Flower, he really was a pathetic-looking article, very small, narrow, no bone and light in condition, I must say that the rest of the stock looked extremely well.

On getting him home, I immediately asked the vet to give him the full treatment - worming, teeth, the lot. My head lad said he looked too weak to lunge so we decided to give him a month with plenty of boiled grub and good hay.

Although he put on precious little flesh from this treatment, he was fresh in himself and good in his skin, so we decided to press on regardless.

When we got to the cantering stage he was still lean and as light as a greyhound, although eating like a bullock. I decided that maybe he would always look like that and intended to ignore his appearance within reason.

In the first two breeze-ups, he appeared unable to go with the others, clearly either useless or bone idle.

However, we persevered and when Greville Starkey came down to get a feel of all the youngsters he said: 'I think this fellow is pulling our legs; he's not doing a tap. When I ride him again would you consider putting a pair of blinds on him?'

This we did and he worked a lot better, although nothing startling. I told my old man: 'I don't think this is any flying machine but let's give him a few runs in sellers and get him placed; then perhaps he'll do for a nursery later on. He's sure to improve because he's such a late foal.' Being so plain, that would, I imagined, be the height of his capabilities.

We decided to run him in a seller at Nottingham on March 28. Greville suggested we put blinkers on and asked could he give him one tap with the whip if he was idling.

He knew full well that both my old man and I were totally against the whip in any shape or form, but we agreed to one flick just to see if the horse was kidding us.

There were eight runners and Doug Smith was on the favourite, trained by Geoffrey Brooke. I said to Greville: 'As you know, we haven't tuned this lad up, but I want to try to find out if he is worth keeping for a nursery. Lay handy and kick on into third or fourth place if you can.'

They're off. Blazing Scent was soon in arrears, with Greville booting and scrubbing but going nowhere. With only a few hundred yards left to run, as a last resort, he gave him one slap. Whoosh! The horse took off and flew past the field as if they were standing still to win by two lengths going away.

I thought to myself: 'What now? Do I let him go if there's a bid, or do I give a few quid to get him back?'

On dismounting, Greville said: 'Although they're a bad lot this lad has got ability and he can only improve.'

Apparently, professional punter Alex Bird, who died only a few months ago, had become very keen on the stopwatch.

He had recorded a fast time for such a race and advised Bill Ball and Bill Carter, two other well-known punters, that the horse should be bought.

For my old man, who did not have a shilling on the animal, anything beyond £300 would have meant a loss. In fact, I went to £650 before dropping out and Carter stepped in with a crowning bid of £700.

The horse went to George Todd to be trained for Ball and Carter, but the trio fell out and Bob Capon, a sporting farmer not averse to a tilt at the ring, took him over.

Each season I expected to see a much bigger, stronger and more robust creature, but not so. He didn't develop at all; in fact, if anything he got lighter in condition with age. Old Horne described him as 'all wire and whipcord.'

Despite this he won 11 races, including the Victoria Cup, when it was run at Newbury after Hurst Park closed down, plus a few decent touches for his owner and trainer.

In a way, I suppose, I was pleased that he hadn't developed physically after I'd had him pinched off me at Nottingham because I always prided myself that my horses looked big and well.

But clearly this lad was born to be an ugly duckling with a great big heart.

Snaffles' best-known title 'Andsome Is Wot Andsome Does' certainly applied to this gutsy, aggressive battler. After his racing days were over, he retired to Bob Capon's farm, along with another useful horse of his called I Claudius.

There the pair of them spent the rest of their days, living off the fat of the land while reminiscing about the touches they had provided for Capon, Todd and fellow punters lucky enough to have been in on the act.

BLAZING SCENT
with a youthful Greville Starkey and
Michael Pope after winning at Nottingham.
He later won a Victoria Cup for George Todd.

FRANK HORNE leads round
Blason, who covered Frigid Flower.

[75]

Just Reward For Speeding

NEARLY FORTY years ago I had the good fortune to train a really delightful filly called Life Sentence, classically bred by Court Martial out of Borobella by Bois Roussel. She had a lot of ability and was a pleasure to handle.

Miss Gladys Yule had purchased her at the end of her two-year-old career from Jeremy Tree at the Newmarket Sales, primarily as a partner for her newly acquired stallion, the Eclipse winner Flocon.

Gladys, together with her mentor cum racing adviser Miss Pat Wolf, were a joy to train for, although ladies with very definite views of their own.

Unfortunately they were besotted with the 'hair in the box' mania, all the rage at the time amongst horsey and doggy ladies. For me a lot of obbery gobbery claptrap, as unlikely to produce a cure as Gipsy Lee's crystal ball.

It was agreed that I should train Life Sentence for the One Thousand Guineas, although it was thought unlikely she would get the mile at Newmarket. The alternative target was the Red Rose Stakes at Manchester on June 6, in those days one of the prestige sprint races for three-year-old fillies.

She ran a very respectable race in the Guineas, making the running until well into the Dip, but it was clear sprinting was her game and the alternative plan would have to be adopted. She was thriving all the

LIFE SENTENCE,
a classically bred filly by **Court Martial** out of a mare by **Bois Roussel.**

time and working extremely well, in fact on seeing the entries for the Red Rose I couldn't pinpoint what could beat her, although she had to concede 17lb to Fair Amazon.

Within a week of the race, and after her last serious gallop, she was looking a picture of health and ready to run for her life. However I had completely forgotten that Gladys had, a week earlier, requested me to pluck a few hairs from the filly's tail and send them to the man with the 'black box' somewhere down in the bowels of the East End, for him to evaluate her well being and start treatment on any hidden defects that might vibrate through to his magic apparatus.

I received what looked like a small roll of toilet paper listing the filly's ailments which, unless treated immediately, would rule out Manchester. In fact, judging by the report she might not survive the night!

I telephoned my vet Percy Male, and read the summary of the report to him. He said: 'What absolute rubbish. I saw the filly only two days ago, she looked a real picture of health, is obviously in peak form, and I would be prepared to give you a certificate to that effect.'

He continued: 'Get on to this geezer, butter him up and ask him to start treatment immediately. He is sure to request more hair, so pluck some from two or three animals other than Life Sentence, plus a few from that cock-tailed old cob of yours for good measure and then, if in fact his machine is capable of recording anything, he'll get into such a bugger's muddle he's sure to report back within a few days that he has cured all the problems. I gave this advice in a similar case a while ago and it worked a charm!'

Sure enough, according to the charlatan he had worked overtime and the filly was now fit to run.

On the morning of the race I was enjoying a very leisurely breakfast after first lot, having booked a seat on a plane to avoid such a long and tiring road journey, plus the fact that I had two speeding offences pending and couldn't afford any more.

At that moment the phone rang: 'Mortons Aviation here, due to thunderstorms en-route we are unable to take you to Manchester today.'

Belting up the stairs to get changed, I shouted to my wife: 'Get my car out will you, and see she's full of petrol, I've got to drive to the smoke and will have to go like the clappers.'

At the time I had the most super regal red Rolls which could really motor but appeared to attract the boys in blue like a magnet. I estimated that I could just about make it in time to declare, due in writing three-quarters of an hour before the race in question.

There wasn't too much traffic on the road and I was just thinking what good time I was making when, approaching Lichfield, the familiar sound of that poxy tinkling bell ranged upsides. There was no point in trying a cock and bull story so I said: 'I'm frightfully sorry officer, I am in a great hurry to saddle a winner at Manchester.'

Showing no signs of relenting he continued to write out a chit, but as I was pulling away he said: 'What was the name of that horse, Sir?'

Having never been to the racecourse in Manchester before I hadn't a clue where the track was situated, but luckily when halted at the next lights I spotted Harry Carr at the wheel of his car upsides. Knowing he was going to the races I latched on to him and, after ducking and diving up back streets at breakneck speed, he went past the entrance marked 'Members of the Jockey Club only.'

I thought 'That's for me,' did a rapid U-turn, brushed the attendant aside and dumped the car in the only available space then ran like hell, pursued by a screaming attendant.

'You've taken Lord Sefton's place and he's coming.' I shouted back 'Bully for him, I'm going.'

With no time to argue, I barged into the weighing room, bawling at the declarations clerk: 'Am I in time for the third race?'

Consulting the clock, he said: 'You've just got two minutes, let me fill in the form - you seem to be in a bit of a state.'

Thank God for that. Now to see if all is well with the filly. At that moment, Pat Healy, my travelling lad, appeared: 'Cutting it a bit fine weren't you guvnor.' In no mood for chip and chaff, I said: 'Never mind about that, is the filly in good shape?'

'Cherry ripe, she was jumping and kicking when she pulled up from her blow out this morning and licked out every oat last night. By the way, there's a spivvy-looking geezer looking for you.'

With that, a dodgy bloke with a long dark overcoat and trilby hat cocked on one side approached me. 'Major, may I have a word. I don't know if you fancy yours, but I've been asked to offer you a monkey to make sure your filly doesn't win.'

Winking, he continued: 'Better than backing her with your own money, eh?'

Already het up and tense, I screamed at him using adjectives I didn't know I was capable of stringing together.

I suppose I should have reported the matter immediately, but nobody had witnessed the conversation and the little creep would have denied the accusation anyway. However, I did intend to point him out to the security fellows if I spotted him again, but from that day to this I have never seen hair nor hide of him again.

When Packham came into the ring I said: 'This filly has never been better, I think she'll glide in.'

In a relieved tone, he replied: 'Thank goodness for that, there was a buzz in the weighing room that you didn't fancy her.'

I stopped him short: 'Get out there, make all and win as far as you like.'

NO MATCH

Only three lined up for the Red Rose Stakes in which Fair Amazon was made an even-money favourite, but she was no match for the speedy Life Sentence.

Life Sentence jumped off well, and raced along easily with Tudor Gem to half-way where Fair Amazon just behind them, already looked in distress. Then Packham sent Miss Yule's filly ahead to win as she liked.

Michael Pope arrived just in time to declare Life Sentence a runner. He had booked a 'plane to the course but the flight had to be cancelled because of thunderstorms. He made a dash by car and arrived exactly two minutes before declaration time.

The young Streatley trainer did well to buy Life Sentence last December on behalf of Miss Yule when Jeremy Tree put her up for sale, because her stud value must be very high.

A daughter of Court Martial and Borobella, Life Sentence comes of one of the late Mr Peter Beatty's most successful lines.

She will next contest the Fern Hill Stakes at Ascot, and, after running at Goodwood, will be retired to her owner's stud at St. Albans to be mated with Flocon.

REPORT from the columns of the Life following the success of Life Sentence in the Red Rose Stakes at Manchester

The result was never in doubt. Life Sentence was always moving smoothly and merely had to lengthen her stride to pull away to win on the bridle by five lengths. I was delighted, not only for Glad's sake, as she had been so keen to win this particular race, but the return of 2/1 against when in my opinion it should have been odds on, was a bonus.

After downing a very large brandy I rang home to tell Kay of our success. Congratulating me, she said: 'You must be exhausted after that hair-raising journey, why don't you stay the night with John at Ingestre. He's about halfway house, shall I give him a ring?'

John, the late Earl of Shrewsbury and Waterford, had a large estate and lived in Ingestre Hall near Rugeley. He was a close friend, had a flat horse with me and a useful jumper with George Owen called Tout A L'Heure on which Dick Francis won a number of races.

I also phoned Glad Yule, who was delighted, but I didn't think she would appreciate the fact that I had been approached to stop her filly and decided to be like dad and keep mum.

On arrival at Ingestre Hall I was greeted by Bill the butler. 'His Lordship is not yet back from shooting but he will be pleased for you to stay the night and has asked me to see to your needs.' Whilst showing me to my quarters, a bedroom big enough for an indoor school with an enormous bathroom about half a furlong down the corridor, he said: 'Dinner will be served at 8.30 but I expect you could do with a bath and a nap meanwhile. I will lay out your dinner jacket whilst you are bathing.' Having explained why I was travelling light, he offered to acquire the necessary gear from the quarters of Major Tony Crofton, John's brother-in-law, with whom I served in the same regiment during the war. His official handle was estate manager, but I rather think he was more of a court jester.

I lay on the bed thinking what a blissful ending to such an eventful day. Little did I know that my problems were not quite over. While squeezing into Tony's dress trousers, which were much too small for me both around the waist and in the crotch, Bill appeared at the door: 'His Lordship sends his compliments and awaits your pleasure in the library for a snort before dinner.'

I filled John in with the events of the day, including the speeding episode. Asking the area in which I was pinched, laughingly he said: 'That's old Bertie's beat. He's shooting here tomorrow - I'll see he's well placed at David's Rock before I twist his arm for you.' Bertie had to be no less than High Sheriff of the County, as those of lesser rank were not invited to blast off from stand four or five at the Rock.

Incidentally, David's Rock was a very famous pheasant drive where King Edward VII is reputed to have shot 91 birds with 93 cartridges. The feat was recorded on a plaque, under which some wag had scrawled 'Bloody Liar'.

Having replaced the top button of my trousers with a safety pin and downed three glasses of excellent giggle juice, temporarily I forgot my discomfort. By now, other members of the local gentry had cast up and we were ushered into dinner. I sat next to my hostess and was getting on famously, in spite of having to manipulate my undercarriage at intervals to avoid strangulation of the testicles.

The pain was now becoming unbearable, so I whispered in the ear of the wench serving at table: 'I'm in real trouble, please get someone to announce that there is a very important telephone call for me.' Apologising profoundly I got out of the room as best I could, but John obviously sensed I was in bother and followed me.

'What's wrong Mike, you're moving as if you had crotch trouble.'

Clutching my lower regions, I replied: 'You can say that again. I feel as if I have a double hernia and my danglers are about to drop off.'

At that moment a waiter passed with a tray of glasses. John shouts: 'Harry, take your trousers off and swop with the Major.'

There we stood in our underpants in the baronial hall, quite an unusual sight but one that caused hilarious amusement when related by our host after the ladies had withdrawn and the port was circulating.

As I sank into the deep old-fashioned feather mattress, tired, happy and full of liquor, I thought: 'Hey ho, what an eventful day, almost worthy of a short story'.

Footnote: To this day I don't know if it was thanks to Bertie or Life Sentence, but I never heard a dicky bird about the speeding charge.

Best Hotel
In Epsom

NIGH ON 40 years ago Edwin McAlpine asked me to train Luxury Hotel. My immediate reaction was one of delight, knowing the horse to be a true stayer with decent form. However, before accepting I said: 'What about Sam Armstrong? He'll have me for breakfast.'

Edwin replied: 'Nay bother, the horse has leg trouble, and Sam says he won't stand training.'

Sam had forgotten more about training racehorses than I ever knew, so what chance did I have? However, Edwin was adamant.

'Pope, old boy, I'd like you to take this fella, I have an ambition to win the Great Metropolitan at Epsom and am confident you and Luxury Hotel can help me to do just that.'

I replied: 'Odd you should have that urge. I used to boast to my mates at school that I would train the winner of the race one day.'

No doubt many people considered the Great Met an ordinary handicap, but for me, and clearly for Edwin, it was a colourful contest with an indefinable characteristic flavour, providing much more fun than a number of boring Group races with minimal fields.

The runners started with their backs to the winning post, raced away in the wrong direction of the course for three furlongs, then swung right-handed through the hurly burly of the fairground, across the open downs, until swinging left-handed onto the racecourse proper about a mile from home.

When we were in our early teens my parents used to hire a large charabanc and encouraged us to invite our school chums for a day out at the races. A picnic for all tastes, plus whelks and jellied eels from a nearby stall for those with the stomach.

I well remember leaning over the ropes which marked the track over common land, and, as the field thundered past like the clappers, the thrill was electric.

That experience made me only more certain that horseracing was for me in some shape or form.

A different sort of thrill was provided by a large, blonde lady billed outside her tented boudoir as Tanner Annie. She drew attention to her charms by chanting 'roll up, roll up, come and see the girl with nothing on but a smile.'

It was a bit of a rip-off at sixpence a go, as she never did reveal all, insisting that it was too cold to remove the bottom half of her woollen bathing costume, despite demands from inquisitive youngsters to 'get 'em off'.

Even so she had lovely violet eyes and a winning smile which revealed a mouthful of gold teeth!

When Luxury Hotel arrived at my yard, his near-fore was so full of heat you could fry an egg on it. The tendon was thick and an ominous shape. To make matters worse he was very heavy-topped, with shoulders like a bull and a backside like a cook.

The only chance was complete rest, so I sent him over to Edwin's stud at Henley with instructions to shut him up in a large box on a ration of hay, wet bran and plenty of doctor green.

Over the weeks the limb responded well and by the turn of the year, although not a pair, the leg was cool, callous and handled well. We decided to press on regardless, as being such a gross devil he would need bags of work and at least a couple of runs before Epsom on April 20.

The first outing was planned for Hurst Park on March 27 where, ridden by Tommy Carter, he ran a cracker and blew like a grampus.

All being well, his second race would be at Windsor on April 5 with Gordon Richards in the plate.

Oddly enough, he started favourite; however, winning the contest was not on the agenda. We had left a bit to work on and success would incur a penalty for Epsom.

In fact he ran a good race, running on like a train to finish second. On dismounting, Gordon said: 'You needn't look any further for a pilot at Epsom.'

We now had a fortnight to bring the horse to peak form. A full-scale bit of work over two miles on Jack Waugh's gallops at Chilton was to be the finale.

I remember Dick Hern, who was with me at the time, setting off with four horses in the box, although I can't remember the names of the other three. Unimportant, but a sign of old age.

I planned to run another horse called Loll, named after his owner, on the same day at Epsom. He, too, had a major chance on his recent form and home work - a big flashy chestnut with four white socks.

He ran in the name of Mr Daniel Nossel, better known on the racetrack as Lolly Clancy - Loll because he was never without a lollipop in his mouth as a kid, and Clancy as that was the nom de plume he used in his boxing days.

He was a likeable little Cockney, who gambled for a living and was probably one of the few professionals who not only won a great deal of money but also died a wealthy man. Unlike most punters, he invested his winnings wisely on the stock market.

I saw him racing the day before Epsom and handed him details of the total commission we wanted him to handle. This included individual bets on both runners, plus an each-way double.

Loll smiled and said: 'Blimey, you'll need to arf inch the bleedin' crown jewels if these two get stuffed.'

The McAlpine family, all members of the vast construction empire and into racing and breeding in a big way, had the most luxurious box, which had been provided for them in return for their expert advice when the stands were redesigned after the last war.

The box accommodated up to 50 people, with a viewing area behind glass, and with tip-up seats like Odeon cinemas.

The luncheons, served by their own staff, usually started with plovers' eggs, smoked salmon and caviar - a far cry from the picnics on top of the bus, and no call for whelks or jellied eels.

The guests were mainly clients, either being feted in gratitude for past favours, or sweetened for future business.

A smattering of friends and titled folk added a bit of flavour, but there was little chance of meeting ladies with violet eyes, gold teeth or short of a bob or two.

However, I did meet the leader of the clan, Sir Malcolm McAlpine, a very dour Scot. He introduced himself saying: 'A word in your ear, laddie. I've been in racing all my life, whilst Edwin is comparatively new to the game. Statistics prove over the years that Epsom is no track for a horse that needs blinkers, has bad legs, or is heavy topped.'

I thought: 'Hell's bells, that's done it. Our fella qualifies on all three counts.' I felt about two feet tall and as debagged as the day I was caught by our parsimonious old headmaster making a book outside the common room.

He dished out a beating and a hundred lines: 'Gambling is a wicked sin - I will never indulge again.' With a smarting backside, but unrepentant, I muttered to myself: 'Do yer wanna bet?'

Entering the paddock as Luxury Hotel walked by, I thought: 'By Jiminy he looks the part and as sharp as a needle.'

Butch Lawson, his devoted lad and minder, turned in for Gordon to mount and said: 'We've won the guineas for the best turned out runner guv, now it's up to Moppy.'

Apparently, Gordon was given that nickname when he entered stables as a skinny little lad with a wild mop of hair.

'They're off', and by the time the runners reached the racecourse proper it was clear Luxury Hotel was only cantering.

Making ground rapidly down and around Tattenham Corner, he sailed into the lead and won by an easy four lengths with Gordon standing up in his irons, a sure sign he had a bundle in hand.

When returning to the winner's enclosure Gordon winked at me and said: 'We needn't have worried about the penalty. He could have won pulling a cart.'

It really was a thrilling climax to a long and precarious build-up for a particular race.

After downing more than my fair share of giggle juice with Edwin and all the other jubilant punters, it was time to go back to work and saddle Loll for the last race.

I told Lester Piggott, then a tall, thin youth of 18, to lie handy and kick on a furlong out, reminding him not to pick up his stick as the horse was extremely nervy. He knew Loll would duck away from the whip as he had won on him as a two-year-old.

Lester was making good ground and going like a winner when he picked up his stick at the distance. Swerving violently to the left, Loll, after losing a lot of ground, ran on again to finish second.

An extraordinary and unprecedented occurrence followed. The stewards, Lord Rosebery, the Duke of Norfolk and Sir Humphrey de Trafford, none of whom was in the first flush of youth, took the unusual course of laying an objection to the horse and charged the jockey with reckless riding.

Together with Lester and a team of other jockeys, I was marched in and asked if I was satisfied with my jockey's riding.

I tried to make light of the incident, not so much to save Lester's skin but to try and save our place double.

To no avail. The stewards suspended Lester for the remaining three days of the meeting and disqualified Loll from second place.

Although Lester disobeyed instructions, in no way was he guilty of reckless riding, and the poor horse merely ducked with fright.

How the stewards arrived at such an extraordinary verdict I will never know. Being the last race, maybe the effect of the Old Tawny was wearing off.

When I came out of the stewards room Loll Clancy greeted me. 'That Lester and those toffee-nosed geezers in there have cost us a bleeding' fortune, but never mind, eh, it's only money!'

That was the sort of man he was - only small but with a big heart.

Luxury Hotel retired to stud at the end of the season. Sadly, he attracted only a handful of ropey mares, so we brought him back into training after nearly three years away from the track.

First time out, looking fit for the fat stock show, he ran at Salisbury in the Carnarvon Cup ridden by the dashing and very competent Bob McCreery. To everyone's complete surprise he won at 25/1.

The old leg now decided that enough was enough and final retirement was the order of the day.

**GORDON RICHARDS (left) who rode Luxury Hotel
and EDWIN McCALPINE (right) the owner.**

**LOLL (Lester Piggott)
is led in by Billy Owen.**

Epsom stewards suspend Piggott

LESTER PIGGOTT was suspended for the rest of the Epsom meeting after riding Loll into second place behind Royal Stream in the last race, the Evelyn Handicap at Epsom yesterday.

The stewards lodged an objection to Loll and the horse was disqualified from second place for crossing.

Many who had backed Westerlands Rosebuds, subsequently placed third for a place on the tote, had left the course before the objection.

Michael Pope, Loll's trainer, who earlier had won with Luxury Hotel: Piggott and several leading jockeys were interviewed by the stewards.

Pope said last night: "The stewards asked me if I was satisfied with the running of Loll. I said I was."

Piggott said afterwards: "It was just a case of Loll swerving."

**PIGGOTT banned :
How the Life
reported the news.**

**A typical scene on a race-day
at Epsom.**

An Eye-Opening Trip To Lewes

WAY BACK in 1960, I received a phone call out of the blue from a fellow, who introduced himself to me as Captain Dudley-Hughes. He asked me if I would train a yearling colt, which he owned in partnership with a Lady Nellie Bewley.

I sensed he could be a nutter or a trainer chum taking the mickey. He prattled on about his colt and suggested we should meet the next day.

Anxious to stall for time, in order to check him out, I said: 'Sorry, but I'm going to Lewes tomorrow.'

In fact, I had no such intention as the horse I was running there wouldn't have won if it had started overnight.

However, he replied: 'Couldn't be better. I've got a runner and will give you a lift down.'

An enormous black Rolls, as long as a hearse and chauffeur driven, swung into the yard.

Upsides, in front, with a burly young redhead at the wheel, was an elegantly dressed and not unattractive middle-aged lady, well adorned with sparklers.

In the back was a swarthy looking gent, smoking a cheroot and sitting on a small tip-up seat. It had to be the said captain.

The chauffeur ushered me into the unoccupied portion of the back seat, the other half being smothered by a dozen or more daily newspapers.

While chatting away about this and that, he told me he was changing his trainer after a disagreement and explained that he always timed his horses when they took part in a gallop.

The previous Saturday at West Ilsley, his stopwatch had failed to operate and the trainer refused his request for a re-run of the trial.

Before I had a chance to wade in, he was banging on the glass window, secluding us from those in the front compartment, shouting: 'Pass the scissors through, Ginger.'

This was obviously a routine request as they appeared without delay and the window was closed immediately.

A frantic searching and rustling of papers followed and suddenly the captain thrust the point of the scissors into the front page with a blood-curdling scream of fury and delight.

This extraordinary performance was repeated three or four times until I could remain silent for no longer. 'May I enquire what you are doing?'

'Of course you may, dear boy. I'm poking the eyes out of the Royals.'

This was clearly a regular pastime as neither the driver nor the lady passenger paid the slightest attention to these bizarre proceedings.

I had already decided that in no way would I ever train for this maniac, nor would I travel home in the same car with him.

Just south of Billingshurst, he tapped on the window again. 'Pull over when you can, Ginger, I need a drink, and my companion looks as thought he could use one too.'

I thought to myself: 'You can say that again.'

Out gets the young chauffeur and, opening the hamper, attempts to draw the cork from a bottle of wine.

He was obviously having difficulty operating a complicated looking corkscrew and enquired: 'Do you know how to operate this tool, milady?'

She replied: 'Yes, Ginger. You stuff it in, give it a good screwing, then pull it out.'

The young man blushed and as I caught Nellie's eye she gave me a broad wink.

Clearly she had embarrassed the poor fellow intentionally.

I thought to myself: Some lady!

By now I sussed that Nellie must be the captain's fancy piece and that Ginger was prepared to exceed his duties as chauffeur if and when required.

Eventually we arrived at Lewes. I thanked Ginger and said: 'With luck you'll have a more peaceful journey home as the Royal Family have all be exterminated.'

He replied: 'I wouldn't bet on it. No doubt we'll be stopping for the evening editions.'

It was a colourless day's racing and I could see I'd be spending my time either dodging the captain and his tart or propping up the bar. The latter was clearly favourite.

**GUY and Di Smith (left),
Fran Leigh and Kay Pope at Clairefontaine to watch Star Bird.**

At that moment, I spotted George Beeby, a very good friend and ever ready for a beverage.

'Come and have a nip, George. I've something to tell you that'll make your hair curl!'

At the bar I asked: What's your poison?' He took a long look at his wristwatch before answering: 'Large scotch and water, old cock.'

I thought to myself: 'Maybe I'm the one that's going bonkers. What does the time have to do with his choice of tipple?'

It transpired that he had a very strict rule. Gin before noon and scotch thereafter, hence the pause for thought at midday.

Having had a good laugh about the destruction of the Royals and a promise of a lift home, I asked George what he was running.

'A sweet little filly in the seller, and I think she'll win.

'Sadly I'm almost sure to lose her because Mrs Graham, the owner, has told me to let her go. I'd like to buy her myself, but I'm a bit stretched for spondulicks at the moment. Come along and help me saddle.'

The filly was a sight for sore eyes, a grand little tit as pretty as a picture but no bigger than a kid's pony.

I decided to have a decent bet and buy her for my wife Kay, whose birthday gift was a month overdue.

Wagon Star, ridden by Eddie Cracknell, duly won by three lengths.

At the subsequent auction, I stood with George and told him I would go to four hundred, but in the unlikely event of 'no bid' I'd be happy to give Mrs Graham the same figure privately.

George agreed but was obviously sad at the thought of losing the filly whilst delighted that I'd agreed to buy her.

'Tell you what, George. You take her home and train her for the last two months of the season.'

His face lit up as he said: 'I shall be absolutely delighted. I can't think of a nicer lady than your wife to train for.'

On the way home in George's old Bentley it was decided we should have a crack at another seller before deciding on her future.

Whilst telling Kay that she was now the proud owner of Wagon Star and had at last got herself a decent trainer, Edwin McAlpine came on the blower.

'I hear you bought the winner of the seller at Lewes today. Was that for me?'

When I explained the position, he said: 'Fair enough. Ask Kay if I can have a half share. Wagon Star can run in her name and I'll pay the training fees.'

We sorted out a race for her at Brighton a month hence. She made all the running and won nicely amidst roars and shouts worthy of an Oaks winner.

It cost 520 guineas to get her back, but everyone was delighted and the champagne flowed.

Being so small, unlikely to grow and the prospects of her training on being remote, we decided to breed from her.

Mollie McAlpine was horrified: 'How extremely cruel. The little girl will only be three years old and a virgin at that. To cover her by some great big beast would be obscene.'

However, reluctantly she agreed after I had promised to attend the ceremony personally and ensure Birdbrook treated the little maiden with gentility and patience.

The following spring the match was consummated without tears and 11 months later a sharp, little grey filly was born.

It was decided by the joint owners that she would be called Star Bird, run in Edwin's name, and be trained in France merely as an excuse to pop over to Paris or Deauville for the odd weekend.

Clive Graham, the Daily Express racing columnist, advised us that Philip Lallie would be a good choice of trainer as he spoke our lingo and was keen on Birdbrook's stock, having trained an extremely useful filly by him called Girl Friend and owned by Desmond Molins.

After a couple of preliminary runs, we were alerted to appear at Clairefontaine, hardly Deauville, but a friendly little track just down the road.

Edwin provided a private aeroplane and together with our great chums, Di and Guy Smith, we set off in festive mood.

On arrival, we met Madame Fran Leigh, the mother of Mick Leigh, a top jump jockey in France.

She was to act as our guide and interpreter for the day. After a wonderful lunch with too much to drink, we gambled on Star Bird with all the francs we could muster.

In a thrilling race, she scrambled into a photo with a horse owned by Ravi Tikkoo and ridden by Scobie Breasley.

The suspense of waiting was intense, but all was well - we had won by the shortest of short heads.

After a further success, it was decided to bring her back to this country and Lallie suggested he should enter her to run over here, as horses from France received the full travel allowance in those days.

The only race for which she qualified before the end of the season was the Challenge Stakes at Newmarket, a race considered way beyond her capability but suitable for the purpose.

To the total amazement and disbelief of all concerned she won at

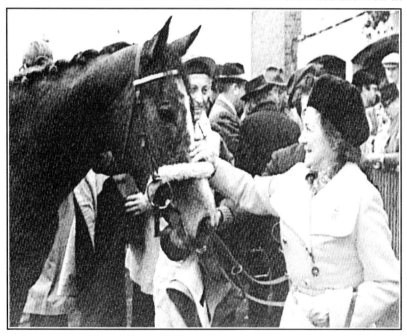

STAR BIRD with her owner
Mrs Kay Pope.

**ABOVE : Star Bird wins
the 1976 Challenge Stakes from Be Tuneful.
BELOW : in winner's enclosure
under French jockey Jean-Pierre Lefevre.**

20/1, ridden by Jean-Pierre Lefevre.

Success in such a prestige race quadrupled her value immediately and the offer we received was too tempting to refuse.

Racing is a funny old game, they do say.

If the captain had not insisted on taking me to Lewes we would not have enjoyed all the pleasure, thrills and financial gains provided by Wagon Star and her daughter Star Bird.

The former bred eight winners in all, but sadly the latter broke her neck in a freak accident soon after joining her new owner in the USA.

By way of a footnote, some three years later a very wealthy industrialist came to see a yearling the BBA had recently purchased on his behalf.

On alighting from a vast Rolls Royce, he said: 'Meet the wife.'

From under a large hat who should appear but none other than the ex-Lady Bewley, with a diamond on her wedding finger the size of a walnut.

With a discreet wink she said: 'Pleased to meet you, Major.'

Trainer By
Royal Appointment

A CAREER with horses was the only profession I was contemplating from a very early age and during the war, while serving with the North Irish Horse in Africa and Italy, a longing for my family and home, plus a few horses to train, provided the incentive to survive.

In my absence, the family worked like beavers to convert a derelict barn and cattle stalls into a stable yard for a dozen or so horses.

This was not as easy as it may sound because all the materials had to be gathered from the back of a lorry or on the black market.

Finally, the wandering soldier returned and, with all hands to the wheel, the conversion was completed.

My neighbours, Frank and Ken Cundell, offered me the use of their excellent gallops, and I'd begged, borrowed or scrounged half a dozen horses to get the show on the road.

They made a motley team: three tubed, one recently fired and another as mad as a hawk and likely to piss off even before the pilot was in the plate.

I told the owner that the filly was a nut case and he asked if there was any cure. Replying with confidence, I said: 'Yes, a bullet.'

He appeared impressed that a fellow so desperate for horses should give such an honest opinion and gave me an order to replace her immediately.

That owner was Edwin McAlpine, who became a great friend and wonderful owner for many years to come.

By now we were geared for action and applied for a licence to train, expecting it to be granted without question in the exceptional circumstances and all requirements laid down in the rule book having been fulfilled.

We could not believe it when back came a letter from Weatherbys, in their customary curt and dictatorial manner, stating that the Jockey Club Licensing Committee would not consider the application because an insufficient number of horses had been listed.

This was a terrible blow to all of us and I went beserk. How could anyone be so cruel and inhuman?

At that moment I really believe my contempt for both the Jockey Club and Weatherbys was greater than my hate for the Germans whom I'd been helping to exterminate on and off for the past three years.

Our plans and dreams had been shattered and the entire operation was in jeopardy. The horses would have to go and the staff be sacked, to say nothing of the damage to my potential livelihood.

I telephoned Cavendish Square at least once a day to let those responsible know what I thought of them.

On one occasion, I spoke to a young lad who said he was only the tea boy, but would like to help if he could. I replied: 'Yes you can help. Stuff some poison in their Typhoo.'

Irresponsible behaviour I know, but it made me feel a great deal better.

While I had been raving and ranting, my wife and mother, a formidable brace of ladies when incensed by injustice to a member of their tribe, had fired off a letter to the reigning monarch, King George VI.

Meanwhile, it had been suggested that I best grovel to the powers that be, a crawling action I had perfected while seeking promotion in the army, as they could be plotting revenge for a successful libel action my old man had brought on my behalf as I was under age at the time of the said offence.

The alleged libel was contained in a notice issued to the Press following a dispute concerning the declaration of a horse called Dormitory, which I was due to bump round in an amateurs' race at the now defunct Gatwick. The defendants were three stewards of the Jockey Club and a clerk of the course.

The hearing lasted three days before Lord Hewart, the Lord Chief Justice, and a special jury in the King's Bench Division.

Mr Gilbert Beyfus KC acted on my behalf and Mr Norman Birkett KC for the defence. The case resulted in my being awarded damages of £200, together with costs.

Experts on law and Press reporters stated that the case was unique in as much as it was the first to succeed against members of the Jockey Club.

If that were so, the position may remain today despite attempts by the Aga Khan and others to dispute their dictatorship.

More likely the true reason for the rejection of my application was the work of an over-zealous clerk sitting on the radiator at 15 Cavendish Square, rigidly adhering to the licensing laws and making decisions without consulting his seniors.

However, no further need for abuse or speculation. Postman Fred, red in the face having pedalled bogwheel over the hill from Streatley, delivered the awaited document.

No explanation, no apology. But never mind, eh? One has learned not to expect such trivialities from the Weatherby regime.

Whether His Majesty's interception influenced events will never be known, but at our celebration party that night we all sang God Save The King, being convinced it was he who sought and achieved fair play on behalf of the Pope entourage.

Off I went hotfoot to the sales with not much money, but bags of enthusiasm. Having been swallowed up time and again when chancing a bid, I suddenly spotted a little grey colt, beautifully put together, full of quality by Lambert Simnel out of Rousslana, and submitted by Mrs Vera Lilley.

The colt attracted little attention, but I loved him and, as he was about to be led out unsold, I raised my catalogue.

After a few bids against the auctioneer he was mine for peanuts, no doubt the minimal reserve to avoid the knacker's yard.

Thrilled with the purchase, I was not in the least envious of the big spenders who had given vast sums for gross, flashy colts displaying their manhood and clearly stuffed with steroids.

The lean little grey fellow would do me. We named him Streatley after the village adjacent to the Pope pound at Wood Farm.

Guy Smith, a close chum since schooldays, agreed under strong pressure to become the proud owner.

It was the first horse he had ever owned and it clearly gave him the taste for ownership as he has never missed a season without a horse or two in training and his colours are still going round 45 years later.

His father, Bert Smith, a grand old boy who farmed in a big way near Bishops Stortford and had grafted hard all his life, didn't believe in throwing money around, said to me: 'If my boy is a big enough bloody fool to blow his cash owning racehorses, that's his funeral. But I don't want him gambling and I feel you could be a bad influence in that respect.'

Little did he know that his son would already bet on flies crawling up a wall if anyone was prepared to lay him. However, that was many moons ago and he is still around punting away on anything that moves for richer for poorer!

STREATLEY (spotted cap), pictured in centre of the Lincolnshire Handicap at the Carholme.

We had the greatest gas with Streatley. He won a number of races, mostly when ridden by apprentices, including one at Wolverhampton when piloted by Henry George, another by Billy Riley at Birmingham and again at Lingfield by Jimmy Palmer.

We also had a couple of cracks at the Lincolnshire Handicap, run on the Carholme at Lincoln in those far-off days.

At the first attempt the little horse was third to Barnes Park and Newton Heath.

The following season, Guy and I went for a decent touch and started backing him ante-post at 100/1 - the day after a very encouraging gallop on Jack Waugh's gallops at Chilton with an animal trained by Frank Cundell called Masked Light. This horse was current favourite for the race.

Streatley ran a super race, being beaten only a length and a half by Phariza, trained by Major Bay Powell.

I remember well noticing the winner walking round the ring before the race with the sweat dropping off his belly and his eyes sticking out like organ stops. 'That one looks as if he's had a bit of ginger,' I remarked to Guy.

In a subsequent race, Phariza was dope tested; this proved positive

**HENRY GEORGE rides his
first and only winner on Streatley at Wolverhampton.**

and Bay was warned off, a decision that many racing folk considered to be an outrage as Bay was totally incapable of such skulduggery.

In fact, the horse had probably been given some help on both occasions, but certainly not by, or with the knowledge of, his trainer.

In hindsight, we were possibly unlucky not to have landed a tidy little tickle for a comparatively small outlay, but the endeavour had given us a great deal of fun and we were still around to punt another day, whereas poor old Bay had lost his livelihood and was never to set foot on a racecourse again.

To conclude on a more light-hearted note, the day after the Lincoln the lad who did Streatley had a black eye.

I enquired the reason and he said: 'I tweaked the young daughter's bum at our digs and her mum gave me a right backhander.'

My travelling lad, who had shacked up at the same lodgings, laughed and said: 'Well, I goosed mother, but she rewarded me with some home-made black pudding for breakfast - not a black eye!'

BEFORE ...

**... AND AFTER : A derelict
barn and cattle stalls become a stable yard for a dozen horses.**

Dick Hern Is My Assistant!

DICK HERN and I were commissioned into the same regiment in the last war and became close friends which we have remained ever since.

Apres la guerre, Dick soon returned to the Porlock Vale Riding School and while he carried out the important task as chief instructor with zest and distinction I fancied his long-term ambition was to break into the racing scene.

We kept in close touch, and by the time I had gathered together a reasonable string of horses, Dick agreed to join me as assistant, a decision neither he nor I have ever regretted.

The first assignment in his new post was to saddle a two-year-old filly called Widow Twankey. She was owned by Lord and Lady Borwick who were present to witness their youngster's first outing.

I went off in the opposite direction to Doncaster with their son George. We thought his horse Teddy Tail had a chance second to none and bet accordingly, while Widow Twankey was having only an airing to confirm she was as moderate as her home work suggested.

The inevitable happened. Teddy Tail was beaten half a length while Widow Twankey pissed up at 20/1. Luckily the Borwicks had been in the game a long time and knew the scene.

Dick was an extremely competent horseman and naturally I was keen to give him some rides in public. My old man and Edwin McAlpine agreed he could ride a lovely little horse they owned in partnership called Sir John IV, a half-brother to the famous Sir Ken.

A loveable character, as kind as a christian, and as nimble as a cat, he was very fond of Dick's sporting little dog, a lurcher called Smokey, who used to jump up and slobber Sir John on the muzzle each time he passed the box door.

Smokey would go onto the gallops and provided he was allowed to bowl along in front of Sir John he would keep going, but if the horse passed him he would duck out and push off home.

Well known in the village, he wandered into people's homes as if they were his own. On one occasion he bounded upstairs into a lady's boudoir and curled up on the bed for the day. When he eventually headed for home he had a pound of sausages in his mouth.

On hearing this story I must say it crossed my mind as to how he was so familiar with the way to the lady's bedroom, unless of course he had accompanied his master on a visit in the past.

It may have been coincidence but there was a short spell when Dick had bangers for breakfast practically every morning!

At long last we found a suitable race for Sir John at Taunton. Dick was all geared up to ride and although the horse clearly had a major chance on the book and was sure to be favourite, he was an exasperating little devil likely to disregard the jockey and run his own race.

Fred Winter won on him one day at Ludlow and on dismounting said: 'He gave me a super ride but the infuriating little bugger totally ignored me.'

Dick Francis and other top jockeys had suffered the same indignity, in spite of which the horse won 17 races and so he must have had a fair idea of what he was doing.

Dick Hern aimed to try and lie handy at Taunton but found himself on the retreat. When all hope appeared to have gone Sir John suddenly picked up, flew his fence, and only just failed to get up.

Being a hot favourite at 11/10 some of the punters were not best pleased. One in particular, a big fat slob, shouted at Dick in a hostile manner: 'Nicely done, captain, you rode that well.'

Not only had he demoted Dick, but he was clearly accusing him of having stopped the horse when in fact he would have given his right arm to win.

A few days later a filly called Must Eat was due to run in an apprentice race at Wolverhampton. I had toyed with the idea of giving the ride to one of my own boys, Bernard Prior, known in the yard as 'Monk' because he was as bald as a coot.

However, he had given Dick a bit of lip on the way to the Downs that morning and was under threat of being hung up on a barbed wire fence by his braces and left there to cool off.

The filly was due to travel up overnight and I had told my travelling lad to declare B Prior unless he heard to the contrary.

That evening, Sam Armstrong rang up to offer the services of his top apprentice Charlie Gaston. I immediately sent a message through notifying the change of pilot.

I flew up with Gordon Richards, but we were very late due to fog, and as I ran to the weighing room I noticed that B Prior was up in the frame, so clearly the message had not filtered through.

The clerk of the scales explained that B Prior had not arrived but there was just time to substitute Gaston who was standing by.

Knowing full well that Prior had never left home, I replied: That's fine. He must have been held up in the traffic.'

Of course, I was an idiot not to explain the facts of the case, but at the time it seemed easier to tell a white lie,

On the stands I told Frank Cundell what had happened and said: Do you think I should ring Dick and mark his card? I wouldn't put it past that shit of a stipe to phone the yard.'

Frank replied: 'Don't be such a prat, a change of jockey is no big deal. Just bluff it out.'

Must Eat was beaten a short head and as we were leaving the stands, the stipe, in an offensive tone, said: 'Pope, the stewards' room for you.'

In I went quite unconcerned, it being a trivial matter, I thought. The chairman of the stewards said: 'Pope, we want you to explain why Gaston rode your filly when Prior was declared.'

I replied: 'As I have already explained, sir, he must have been held up by traffic.' I thought to myself: 'More likely by barbed wire!'

He looked about to burst: 'Very interesting, I'm sure. Our stipendiary steward telephoned your stables at Blewbury and a Major Hern said Prior was in the yard doing his horses.'

'Gordon Bennett, that's goosed it!' I tried to explain that there had been no ulterior motive, but they didn't want to know and ordered that the case be referred to the stewards of the Jockey Club.

On returning home, I found poor old Dick in quite a state, having sensed by the mysterious phone call that he may have unwittingly dropped me in it.

Off I went to Newmarket to face the music. Marched in like a small schoolboy about to be thrashed, I only wish I'd had the guts to drop my trousers and bare my bum just for the hell of it.

However, they threw the rule book at me and announced that after lengthly deliberations my licence would not be withdrawn, but the maximum fine of £100 would be imposed.

The other case that day concerned the mighty Captain Cecil Boyd-Rochfort, who trained for the Queen. He suffered the same fine for an alleged non-trier.

Apparently, the pacemaker for a very long odds-on favourite in a stayers' race had gone a bit too well and the poor unfortunate stopping jockey had had great difficulty anchoring it.

At least I was in the best company as we were the first two to suffer the maximum penalty.

Two more suitable races were coming up for Sir John, one at Huntingdon. Sir John looked a picture and at 4/1 was a knocking bet provided he was in the mood.

Turning out of the back straight he appeared to have no chance, but once again picked up, flew the last three fences and won nicely.

The press report stated: 'Major Hern, who had been riding a patient and well-judged race, brought Sir John along with a strong run and in the end was not all out to win quite comfortably.'

I bet old Sir John would have had a good laugh if he could have read that report!

A fortnight later at Stratford he was a warm favourite and two well-known farmer brothers, Les and Al, both fearless punters but like most gamblers inclined to talk through their pockets, said: 'If your jockey can ride, yours is a certainty.'

Running his usual race from behind, Sir John sets Les off: 'Your pilot must think the horse can sprout wings.'

At that moment Sir John puts in a terrific leap and away he goes. Al joins in: 'How far would he have won with a jockey up?'

Skipping over the last two fences, the horse was really motoring and as one the brothers chant: 'He'll win now. Get in there, my son.'

Turning to me, all smiles, they said: 'That's some sort of pilot of yours. He timed it just right.'

Dick has now been part of the team for nearly four years and a girl called Sheilah Davis is receiving a lot of attention. Finally she gets the bachelor boy to name the happy day and marches him off to be spliced.

There were a lot more fun and frolics for a further 12 months until Dick landed the job as private trainer to Major Lionel Holliday at Newmarket. We were all thrilled that he had finally gained an entry to the big time.

From that day to this, in spite of a terrible hunting accident, the gallant Major has been winning all the top races, including 25 classics, but I dare say he still remembers the fun and intrigue provided by Sir John IV, Teddy Tail, Brawby Lad, Cephalonian, Dusty Grey and a few more old plugs, especially those destined for a gamble in sellers,

> Then Major W R Hern, who had been riding a patient and well-judged race, brought Sir John IV along with a strong run, and in the end was not all out to win fairly comfortably from Southern King, with Don Kerry a good third.
>
> M Pope deserves special congratulations for the manner in which Sir John IV was turned out, this good-looking half-brother to Sir Ken still having a summer coat and carrying a mass of muscle, while his mane and tail had been plaited by an expert.

How the Life's Tom Nickalls reported Sir John IV's win on the day Sir Ken showed even greater brilliance

which we camouflaged with bowed tendons, curbs, and other ailments in order to bamboozle potential purchasers and over-enthusiastic auctioneers.

However, at the end of the day, I am sure Dick will agree that Sheilah has proved to be the best winner of them all.

**DICK HERN (on Dusty Grey), was with the author
for some five years before he got his big breakwith Major Lionel Holliday.
BELOW : Teddy Tail (nearest of the trio) Cephalonian
and Sir John IV work on the Downs.**

Jumping
For Joy

AT NEWBURY races one day I had the good fortune to meet Colonel Sam and Mrs Eve Green, a charming couple who were shortly to join my team of owners. They were a sporting crowd who raced purely for fun and the Greens were to prove no exception.

Sam said he would like me to buy him a horse, preferably a staying chaser. His ambition was to have a runner at the Cheltenham Festival.

He indicated a figure of around £5,000 which, of course, ruled out the ready-made article. It would be a question of finding a young horse with plenty of potential.

The horses-in-training sale at Newmarket was shortly coming up and I had marked off a grand sort of horse which I'd seen run second on the Flat. I had made a mental note at the time not to miss out if ever he came on the market.

He was a big, strong, brown gelding by Tanerko out of Chatting by Arctic Star, with a lot of bone and the ideal stamp for a chaser. Only four, he was in need of more time before contemplating fences.

At the time he was ante-post favourite for the Manchester November Handicap and was to be offered for sale with the engagement - a sprat to catch a mackerel. With that added incentive, he would probably fetch between five and ten grand.

However, a blabbering blacksmith had heard the boss say that heat and filling had flushed up just below the near-fore knee following a recent gallop.

Both trainer Arthur Budgett and his horse doctor Charles Frank were good friends of mine and I knew that in confidence they would mark my card. They assured me the problem was minor and nothing rest wouldn't cure.

By sale time the legs handled well, although still not quite a pair. No doubt the dogs had been barking because a number of those examining the horse went straight for his near-fore, running their hands down the leg again and again.

He was knocked down to me for 4,800 guineas and before you could say 'How's yer father', the Jonahs, who frequently bid but seldom buy, hastened to assure me I had dropped a clanger.

That evening I phoned Charles Frank and told him I'd bought Tantalum. His immediate reaction was encouraging: 'Well done, you've got yourself a bloody nice horse. Give him three or four weeks on the roads and then press on."

Not giving Sam much chance to back off, I said: 'If we haven't fallen off the perch by then this fellow could be your Cheltenham challenger.' Excitedly, he replied: 'All right, I'll have him, but don't tell Eve what I paid.'

We decided on a few runs on the Flat, then a season's hurdling before progressing to fences. The following season on the level he ran six times, was placed in all of them and never had a hard race or a slap round the tail.

Without doubt an exciting prospect for the jumping game, he did not escape the attention of many trainers, who made tempting offers, but Sam and Eve were on cloud nine and not in the mood to talk turkey.

The following season, from the time we popped him over a bundle of faggots, we knew we were in for some fun and frolics. He ran ten races in all, winning six, one of which was a two-mile Flat race at Ascot, ridden by Pat Eddery. My own lad Barry Davis, who incidentally was also a Frenchie Nicholson product, rode him in all bar one of the hurdle races, while the amateur Falcon Collings won on him at Sandown.

Sam and Eve never missed seeing their horses perform and we had numerous happy and hilarious days out, with the boot of the car stuffed with picnic hampers and bottles of booze. Sam couldn't resist a cut at the bookmaker, but was a very sporting loser and never bemoaned his luck.

Eve, born and bred in Ireland, couldn't resist an antique shop in spite of Sam's insistence that their home already resembled an over-stocked museum.

Passing through Broadway on the way to the races, she haggled for a small bureau costing the thick end of a monkey. With a wink, she whispered in my ear: 'Don't tell Sam what I paid.'

Now for the day of reckoning. Would Tantalum take to fences? Personally, I was confident, which no doubt influenced my judgement. I put Barry Davis on Tantalum and one of the lads on the lead horse. Although a useful pilot, Barry had little experience over fences.

Jumping slowly and deliberately with little enthusiasm, Tantalum negotiated the obstacles, but only just. Frank Cundell watched the dismal performance with me and when I said: 'Well, what the hell do you make of that?' he replied: 'If you want my honest opinion, Barry is not forceful and experienced enough for the job.'

Respecting Frank's judgement, as always, I went straight home and phoned David Nicholson, known to one and all as the Duke.

Having told him the score, he agreed to come over first lot. It was a foul morning, pissing with rain and blowing a gale, and far from ideal conditions for either man or beast.

The fences were on the collar and before turning in to face the first flight the horses disappeared from view, but the moment they reappeared Tantalum was into his bridle.

With a meaningful roar, 'Get in there my son' from David, the horse cocked his big ears, outjumped the lead horse, and galloped on over the next two fences as bold as brass.

When they trotted back David winked at me and said: 'That'll do guvnor. I'd ride him over fences tomorrow on any track you like.'

For his chasing debut we chose a two-mile novice at Windsor. I told David he could ride the horse in all his races if he fancied him, but made it absolutely clear I would not stand for whip-happy cowboys.

TOGETHER at the last,
Tantalum (David Nicholson, right) jumps with
Statfold Monty (Ron Barry), who came down seconds later,
leaving the Pope horse to come home 15 lengths clear.

In the paddock, I asked him: 'What will you do?', meaning how would he ride the horse. He replied: 'I shall qualify him for the Totalisator Champion Chase at Cheltenham in March.'

With Sam and Eve present, I didn't express my feelings aloud but thought to myself: 'Cheeky bugger, the horse hasn't jumped a fence in public yet. No wonder they call him the Duke.'

Qualify! I'll say he did, and in some style too. Making practically all, he won by 30 lengths. Sam and Eve were over the moon. The mere mention of Cheltenham brought music to their ears and the Duke was now the blue-eyed boy.

The preparation for the big time was going according to plan. Tantalum won a couple more chases and was improving all the while. On the day, I took a chance and told Sam to have a good old-fashioned banco, something I was loathe to do as, given the least encouragement, he would bet like a drunken sailor.

On this occasion, however, he said: 'I'm so excited I don't think my old ticker will stand the added strain of a large bet. All I want to do is win the race.' There was of course five grand added to the stakes, which was big money over 20 years ago.

Sam, Eve, my wife Kay and I watched the race together. It was a thrilling contest. Our fellow jumped from fence to fence and with the Duke riding a very stylish race, hugging the inner and keeping his powder dry until after the last, he kicked on up the hill to win by 15 lengths.

The cheers and applause from my party were nothing compared with the tremendous roars from Pat Eddery and Billy Sargison, who were watching together close by.

Billy, the lad who did Tantalum, had already won the prize for the best turned-out horse. Pat, no doubt, had to scoot off over Cleeve Hill back to Frenchie Nicholson's yard in time for evening stables.

On returning to the winners enclosure, David acknowledged a rousing reception with his customary broad wink and touch of his cap.

The excitement was intense. Eve was crying with joy and, looking a million dollars, stepped forward to receive the trophy, while Sam stood proudly by chatting to the overjoyed Di Nicholson, who looked odds on to win a prize for the best dressed lady on the day.

Away to the bar, where a jubilant Colonel entertained the world and his wife, including a team of Eve's comrades from over the water.

**A delighted Eve Green (right)
receives the Totalisator Champion
Chase trophy after Tantalum's win in 1971.**

2441 Totalisator Champion Chase £4,246·50 (£1,272; £611; £280·50)
3m 100yds   3-5 (3-14)

2173³TANTALUM 7-11-7 D Nicholson *(chased ldr led last, rdn out)* 1
2282²HALLY PERCY 7-11-0 T Biddlecombe *(steady hd-wy 14th, lost pl 17th,*
  r.o wl flat) .... 15—2
1937³TUSCAN PRINCE 7-11-7 P McLoughlin *(led to 2 out, wknd last)* .... 3—3
2248*CHARLIE H 9-11-7 J Haine *(lw, nvr near to chal)* .... 4—4
2280 LUCKY EDGAR 6-11-3 J Woodman *(mistakes, bhd when hmpd 17th,*
  r.o flat) .... 25—5
2067*ORIENT WAR 8-11-7 T Murphy *(lw, ev ch 16th, wknd 17th)* .... hd—6
1951*PRINCESS CAMILLA 6-11-7 M Gifford *(a bhd)* 7
2201*ARGENT (fav) 7-11-7 R Coonan *(f 9th)* 0
2255⁴BAY TUDOR 6-11-7 B Brogan *(prom to 15th, p.u bef 17th)* 0
2062*DAD'S LAD 8-11-7 T. Stack *(prom to 14th)* 0
2266 MILL MELODY (H) 8-11-7 John Williams *(prom till f 9th)* 0
1925³MOON STORM 8-11-7 J Cook *(bhd when f 3rd)* 0
2130*SAN MIGUEL (H) 8-11-7 G Thorner *(prom to 15th, wkng when f 17th)* 0
2335 STATFOLD MONTY 7-11-7 R Barry *(held up, 2nd and ev ch when f last)* .. 0
2287²KING TUDOR 7-11-3 B R Davies *(bhd when f 9th)* 0
2332 TE FOU 8-11-3 A Turnell *(t.o 15th, p.u bef 17th)* 0

11/8 Argent *(tchd 15/8),* 6 O War *(tchd 4's),* 15/2 Charlie H, 11 H Percy, 12 T
Prince *(op 10's),* 13 M Storm *(op 10's),* 14 TANTALUM *(ap 12's tchd 16's),* 15 S
Miguel *(op 12's),* 25 D Lad, L Edgar, 33 o. (16 ran).

M Pope *(Col S W Green), Streatley, Berks.*   Breeder—H H Renshaw.

Tote—£1·82 Pl 38p, 30p, 23p *Time—6/43s* (a33).

**WHO ELSE KNEW? The 14-1
success of Tantalum in the Tote Champion Chase
as recorded by Raceform Up-To-Date.**

Paddy fell down and Patrick got drunk but nobody cared. The big horse had won and it was all such gas.

A grand day to be sure. Sam had achieved his ambition, and Eve was just happy for him. God bless those lovely people.

Before penning this memorable day, I had a word with David to help me refresh my memory on a couple of points.

He said: 'I must tell you something I have kept to myself since that day I came over to school on the downs that filthy morning over 20 years ago.

'When out of your view and before we turned into the first fence, I gave Tantalum a couple of cracks on his backside because he wasn't paying attention. Into his bridle he went and then away, jumping like an old hand.'

On pulling up, Barry Davis said: 'Don't tell the guv'nor you gave the horse a slap. He'll go bonkers and jock you off.'

David continued: 'I promise you that was the first and last time I gave him one down the backside.'

BILLY SARGISON and Sam Green
both agree that Tantalum is something special.

Cagnes Coup Ends
All At Sea

EVERY WINTER for many years my wife and I spent two or three weeks in the South of France as guests of our owners and very close friends, Edwin and Mollie McAlpine.

We flew over in their private jet and enjoyed a happy holiday eating, drinking, gambling and sleeping.

Each February and March many racing folk headed for the sun, reclining somewhere along the Cote d'Azur between Monte Carlo and Cannes. On entering the casino the scene was not unlike the owners' and trainers' bar at Cheltenham or Ascot.

Around the mid-sixties it was becoming the done thing to take horses down to race at Cagnes-sur-Mer, near Nice. The track was unique, with a view from the stands reaching away out over the blue Mediterranean.

More than once Edwin had suggested we should join the spree, but I managed to dissuade him, saying that he didn't have the right type of animal, or trainer for that matter!

We seldom crawled into bed much before first light, surfacing to take a beverage before strolling along the croisette for a lingering luncheon.

Then it would be back to bed for a siesta before returning to the factory and a further session at the tables.

The thought of driving to the racecourse at sparrow fart to supervise a few moderate horses belting round a dirt track, followed by cafe noir and croissants in the lads' hostel stinking of French tabac and garlic, was not, to my mind, an attractive alternative.

However, Edwin was not to be denied and said: "Well, if I don't have the right sort of horse, can you buy me half a dozen that are?"

Frankly, I hadn't a clue what type of animal was required, but agreed to purchase an assortment at the Tattersalls horses-in-training sale the following autumn.

In those days, stabling was very limited for horses trained outside France, and when I applied they had all been allocated.

Saved once again, I thought. But no, Edwin had spotted an advertisement in The Sporting Life. Arthur Thomas, who trained near Warwick, had booked more than he needed and would be pleased to transport and prepare horses to run at the Hippodrome.

I managed to buy four horses and it was agreed they would join Arthur's yard early in the New Year to be schooled over French-type hurdles before being boxed down to the sunny south.

A young jockey called Martin Blackshaw had been doing most of the schooling and I suggested he be given a small retainer to ride them both in their work and races. This was preferable, I thought, to a variety of French coachmen, who couldn't speak our lingo and might be too free with their batons!

We had a hilarious flight over. The first cork blew off before we were airborne, when the pilot announced that Fad, a horse of ours on which we'd had a good punt at Nottingham that afternoon, had won at 9-1. The holiday really took off.

On leaving Nice airport, we called at the racecourse en route to Cannes only to discover that all bar one of our nags were temporarily out of action. And there was more. Arthur had fallen out with Martin Blackshaw and sacked him.

However, Rainbow Lad was said to be ripe and ready for the big race of the day on the following Sunday. He had already run once to get a feel of the track and the frog pilot had expressed himself well pleased, indicating that he would win next time out.

We all arranged to meet for an aperitif on the Carlton terrace before setting off for luncheon on the racecourse.

George Beeby was missing, so I nipped up to his room and a rather pathetic voice came from the bathroom: "Mike, old cock, I need help. I'm cast in the bath and, what's more, some rotten bugger has filched all my cash during the night."

In fact, he had been extremely lucky at the chemmy table, calling and winning some big banks when unaware of their value due to his long absence from the casino.

Sensing that disaster might be imminent, we persuaded him to deposit his profits with the hotel banque and push off to kip after a few jars for the road.

The following morning the concierge, clearly an agent for the local bookmakers, agreed to handle our commissions. In rare holiday mood, three car-loads of racing folk set off to cheer home Rainbow Lad.

Edwin had booked a table for our party of 12 in the racecourse restaurant and we enjoyed an excellent luncheon.

As the runners went out for the first race, we noticed the stewards preparing to climb up into the crow's nest. There was an attractive lady in their midst who Arthur explained was the equivalent to our stipendiary steward.

The male members of the party stood back like true gentlemen to allow the lady to ascend first, but as she climbed the iron ladder, we noticed that instead of averting their glance, they raised their eyes as if having a quick peep up her skirt.

I mentioned this fact to Arthur and laughingly he said: "Oh, yes! While the stewards are having lunch, the male stipe makes a book as to the colour of the knickers she will be wearing.

"Last week he scooped the pool because it was a hot day and she wasn't wearing any at all!"

Now for the Grand Prix de Monte Carlo. In the paddock I said to the jockey, pointing to his whip, a ghastly looking weapon some three-feet long with enormous flaps on the end: "We don't like the stick. Comprenez-vous?"

With a sadastic grin, he replied: "Oui, monsieur, you like plenty of stick?"

Clearly, he had mistaken my orders and was now at liberty to knock spots off our poor little devil. However, Martin Blackshaw assured me he would have a quick word to clarify the position.

They're off and Rainbow Lad goes straight to the front. Urged on by shouts and roars from the crowd of inebriated English supporters, he continued to bowl along at the head of the field.

When the German runner drew up to his girths on the turn, away he went again. Finally, the commentator, with voice at fever pitch, shouted: "Victoire pour les Anglais."

The excitement was contagious and we all flocked to the winner's enclosure surrounded by Press jabbering like vultures hungry for a story.

The jockey kissed Mollie, dislodging her hat. And the photographers took pictures of the event from every angle.

As the presentation was about to be performed, amidst mountains of mimosa, suddenly there was an ear-piercing blast on a horn followed by the dreaded word "Objection." Immediately the mood of entente cordial changed to one of hostility.

Edwin and I barged into the weighing room just in time to witness the two jockeys concerned screaming abuse at each other in their respective tongues while waiting to be interrogated by the stewards.

Eventually they re-appeared and we understood our jockey to say that he had lost the race for using the whip too much.

I flew at him in a rage: "You bloody little frog. I told you not to hit the horse." I was about to take a poke at him when an interpreter intervened.

"Non, non, he didn't hit your horse. He struck the German jockey across the face in the final turn."

Threatening never to return, we stormed out of the weighing room in disgust. I reminded Edwin that we had to pay the bill before leaving.

Faced with l'addition, a blank look came over his face. "I can't pay the bill, old boy. Can you help?"

The mood changed yet again and amid roars of laughter, the entire party managed to scratch together just enough to pay.

The waiter failed to see what was so funny as there was Sweet Fanny Adams left for him.

Most of the party were skint and, economising, gave the casino a miss that evening, settling for an omelette au natural or an oeuf en gelee in their room.

But, as usual, my old mucker Guy Smith couldn't resist a little dabble and kidded me on to join him.

Behind the brass rail and a mountain of chips was Harvey Leader, the well known and popular Newmarket trainer.

He had clearly dined out well and said: "Come and join me boys. This is like taking candy from a baby."

The Duke of Norfolk, who was sitting near to him, was clearly not amused.

A glance at the financial state of the other players and the croupier announced: "Le parti finit."

Harvey, having cashed his chips, stuffed wads of francs into his pockets and insisted we join him for a night cap at the Moulin Rouge.

We groped our way into a dimly lit dive, seething with bodies of every colour and creed. A bottle of champagne was produced by a near-naked lady into whose garter Harvey stuffed a fist full of francs saying: "Help yourself out of that lot, sweetie."

This gesture prompted a striptease by the dual-purpose maiden, of breeding unknown and with plenty of mileage on the clock.

HARVEY LEADER   **ARTHUR THOMAS**

She appeared to direct her act at Guy, who looked somewhat embarrassed, but soon warmed to her charms when, stark naked, she sat herself down on his lap.

With Harvey's cash rapidly evaporating and my old school chum over-heating, I sensed it was time we called a cab. Strong disapproval was short-lived when casually I happened to mention it was a pity their wives Di and Miriam were not present!

THE well appointed racecourse at Cagnes-sur-Mer set against a back-drop of the sunny Mediterranean

MARTIN BLACKSHAW

In the morning, around the pool at the Majestic, Mollie asked if we had enjoyed ourselves at the casino.

Guy glared at me as if to say: "You dare." Harvey coughed and asked Miriam if she would like to go shopping.

Rainbow Lad returned home and after a short rest won at Windsor, ridden by Paul Cook.

The others ended up either as "boeuf en croute" on the menu at the Negresco, or outside the hotel on the cab rank, drowsing in the sunshine in woollen nightcap with bobbles on, awaiting a client for a clippety-clop along the croisette.

Some may say what a sad ending but, come to think of it, probably better than getting slapped round the bum with a whip when already doing your very best.

Getting Ahead With A New Hat

IN THE mid-sixties when I was training at Streatley, yearlings bred or purchased by my loyal and long-suffering owners were trained as two-year-olds mainly by Frank Cundell, with odd ones by his cousin Ken, George Beeby or Sam Armstrong.

It was agreed that if the youngsters displayed ability and looked like training on at the end of their first season they would come to me as three-year-olds.

The purpose of this arrangement concerned the gallops. While ideal for older horses, the distance from my yard was a long haul for immature two-year-olds.

All the owners involved were close friends and the scheme worked amicably and well.

In 1964, Guy Smith and Edwin McAlpine were offering their yearlings at the October Sales, two of which had to be withdrawn.

One of Guy's, a small brown filly by March Past out of Bienfaisant by Chanteur II was a flighty little bitch just like her mother.

She could kick the eye out of a needle and was as stubborn as a mule. When attempting to load her into the horsebox the handlers were given a very rough time. She reared upon the ramp, fell over backwards and broke loose.

With the lead rein wrapped around her hock, she set off across the Cambridgeshire countryside like hell out of the night, finally being cornered an hour and a half later looking as if she had run into a tribe of Red Indians, who had skinned her alive.

Of course, she had to be withdrawn from the sale and remained in her box for three months, proving lethal at both ends.

The young vet, who ventured to give her an injection and dress her wounds, ended up crouching in the manger awaiting a chance to break cover while pretending to look unconcerned.

Early in the New Year, it was decided to send the filly, now named French Parade, down to Frank's yard at Aston Tirrold.

All the Smith entourage and assorted staff were armed with various weapons of encouragement to assist with the loading. Eventually, however, vet Peter Rossdale had to be called to inject a mammoth dose of tranquillizer before the filly could be manhandled into the horsebox.

Meanwhile, Edwin's filly, a butty little grey by Welsh Abbot out of Froment by Vilmorin, now named Welsh Harvest, was about to join Sam Armstrong. She too had missed the sales, having been pricked by the blacksmith.

I refrained from enquiring after French Parade as Frank frequently replied: "What! That bloody little cow."

You could hardly blame him because his head man, vet, and any lad brave or daft enough to get within striking distance of the filly had suffered some form of indignity or other.

Welsh Harvest however, was pleasing Sam immensely, having run a couple of places at Windsor and Brighton.

He enthused: "She is a charming little filly in every respect and will win races without a doubt. In fact, I'd like to run her at Ally Pally on May 25. Lester will ride and they will take all the beating."

A short while later Frank gave me a buzz to say: "French Parade is starting to become quite civilised and I've really taken to her in spite of all her idiosyncracies. With a bit of luck she could have a breeze up at Ally Pally on May 25."

Off we set for my favourite racecourse, where Welsh Harvest won very comfortably. But surprise, surprise, who was second of the 22 runners? None other than French Parade, with Greville Starkey at the controls, and running on like a train at 20-1.

Welsh Harvest went on to run another six times that season, winning four more times and being second twice.. In three of these events, French Parade finished well behind and on the form book was clearly not within a stone of the grey.

However, they were to clash yet again at Chepstow on August 30, with only two other contenders, and it looked a foregone conclusion for Welsh Harvest.

All concerned, including Guy, Di and myself, decided to accept Edwin and Mollie's invitation to luncheon in their sumptuous box at Epsom rather than flog all the way down to Chepstow to witness a procession.

When the time for the Chepstow race was approaching Mollie rang Sam Cowan's to listen to the commentary. As she put down the phone Edwin enquired: "How far did Welsh Harvest win?"

With a long face, Mollie replied: "She didn't win. Some horrible little beast called French Parade slaughtered her."

Rather an embarrassing situation for Di and Guy as obviously they were bursting to explode with enthusiasm. However, they had to curb their joy, being guests of Edwin and Mollie, who momentarily had clearly forgotten who owned the so-called "horrible little beast!"

Towards the end of October, Frank said that French Parade had broken in her jacket and was over the top for the season.

He suggested she should run in a Newmarket nursery to get a few pounds off her back in readiness for the following year and then be dropped off after the race at Guy's Manor Farm Stud at Thriplow on the way home.

From my point of view, I hoped she would finish nearer last than first, and in Frank's absence I told Paul Cook the filly was past her best and to be very kind to her.

This he was, but even with top weight she weaved her way through her 25 rivals to get up and win a head on the line.

None of us had a tossing coin on her, as the price of 100-8 suggests. However, I had to join in the celebrations because Di and Guy were obviously thrilled to have a home-bred winner at their local track and to hell with the prize-money, betting, handicapper, or anything else.

The two fillies, now both finished for the season, had won eight and been placed in nine other races between them; in fact, neither had been out of the frame in a total of 17 races.

Both came to my yard at the turn of the year. French Parade had wintered extremely well and was clearly on the upgrade, whereas I feared Welsh Harvest had become very disenchanted with the game and had not developed.

Being a magnanimous sort of fellow, I suggested Sam should keep the filly. However, he insisted on honouring our agreement, a very sporting gesture but one that only strengthened my doubts!

We would have to persuade the handicappers to drop French Parade by at least a stone, whether by fair means or foul. If she produced no early form they might consider she had failed to train on, or had deteriorated under a new and comparatively inexperienced trainer.

In those days trying to outwit the team of Jockey Club handicappers was in my opinion the most intriguing and skilful part of the training profession.

One would enter an animal in four or five handicaps up and down the country from Folkestone to Bogside, each of which was served by a different handicapper.

Every Friday morning there was a mad rush to grab the Racing Calendar from the postman to see which of the handicappers had either made a cock-up or taken the most lenient view. No matter where that particular race was the animal had to take part merely to confirm the assessment.

Provided the owners and jockeys were willing to go along with this slightly devious but essential charade, the animal concerned could drop ten or more pounds fairly quickly.

Today the rating system is much more sophisticated and less corrupt, bobbing up and down a pound or two with each run. Fairer, they say, but in my opinion boring and nowhere near such fun!

At the beginning of the following season, I put French Parade in a race at Newbury over her wrong trip and on ground which turned against her.

However, with 9st 6lb on her hump and short of a race, she had no chance. I told Frankie Durr: "Everything is against her so treat her with tender loving care."

Running a blinder she was always handy and got beaten a neck.

Undoubtedly, she could have won with a hard race but, being a temperamental filly, we never allowed her to be touched with a whip and Frankie had carried out his instructions to the letter.

I said to Guy: "Now that really has put the cat amongst the pigeons. Where the hell do we go from here?"

However, the filly was obviously still improving both in ability and temperament, so we decided to have a cut at the Stewards' Cup, but not before she had won a five-furlong handicap at Sandown from Polyfoto (gave 21 lb).

She ran a cracker under a 10 lb penalty at Goodwood, ridden by Fred Messer claiming the seven, yet another Frenchie Nicholson protegee. Looking all over the winner, she got beaten half a length by Ron Smyth's Patient Constable in the last few strides.

Scanning the programme book for possible targets, I spotted two in three days at the Ascot September meeting. Meanwhile, there was a lesser event at Yarmouth which I thought she could win without much trouble. Win she did and in the most impressive style.

I broke the news to Di and Guy that I wanted to run at Ascot on the Thursday. Guy said: "Isn't that a bit out of our depth?"

SAM ARMSTRONG,
who trained Welsh
Harvest and other
two-year-olds for
the author.

Whereupon Di chipped in: "Don't talk such rubbish. I love Ascot and will buy a stunning new hat for the occasion."

Continuing, I said: "Get yourselves ready for another shock. I plan to leave the filly at Ascot and run her again on the Saturday."

Bursting with good cheer, Di exclaimed: "Oh, how marvellous. That'll mean another new hat."

Guy intervened: "Farming won't stand all these new creations."

In half a whisper, Di retorted: "Mean old sod, he's as tight as a duck's bum."

On the Thursday, French Parade won the Buckingham Palace Handicap competently ridden by Fred Messer.

FRENCH PARADE (Fred Messer)
beats Polyfoto at Ascot

Di, looking like a milliner's model, swooped to the winning enclosure to make quite certain all her friends and others were given every chance to view her head-gear.

I was assured by all the experts that we had no chance of beating Polyfoto at a difference of only 5lb on the Saturday in the Star and Garter Stakes. However, French Parade, ridden by the same boy, made all.

Di also got the double up. Her hat was a sight for sore eyes, although not infringing the Duke of Norfolk's guidelines, and she announced her intention to run all her horses at Ascot in future. Sadly, they didn't cater for selling platers at this venue!

However, we soon lowered our sights and two days later pushed off to Nottingham to cheer home Messer on 20-1 Blase Simon, owned by our mutual friend Randall Knight.

I didn't notice any startling titfers, but the champagne tasted just the same!

Ditty That Went For A Song

WHEN I retired from training my loyal and long suffering team of owners, all close personal chums, asked me to look after their future racing interests.

This very sporting gesture I was, of course, delighted to accept, being anxious to remain involved with the racing game and those with whom I had enjoyed working (and conniving) with for many happy years.

Around that time the virus had become widespread, knocking out entire yards for weeks on end. It was for this reason that I advised Edwin McAlpine, who always had about a dozen in training, that he should spread his string with four or five different trainers.

By doing this it would hopefully mean that at least some of his horses would be free of the plague to provide him with a bit of sport throughout the season.

Although Edwin worked extremely hard he loved to go racing a minimum of once a week — winter and summer — and have as many runners as possible.

In the autumn of 1977, the home-bred yearlings had been named and were about to go out to their various trainers.

Mainly, these were of the old school, who still viewed ownership as a rich man's hobby, and entertained them and their racing managers accordingly.

The sales were approaching and Tom Jones rang to ask if I thought Mr McAlpine would be interested in buying a yearling.

I explained that although Edwin never gave a firm order for one he seldom declined an offer to take over an animal bought on spec or surplus to requirements, especially if I had given him a nudge.

I never quite understood the basis of this theory, but it seemed to work. In fact, only the season before we had taken over a yearling which Tom had purchased on spec for 5,000gns. Bobby Dolbey had been given the first option, but was horrified by her rather weird forelegs and ducked out.

This filly by Sallust was christened Saltation and she did us proud, winning a number of races and producing some useful winners as a broodmare, including Imperial Salute.

When the sales were finished Tom rang me to say he had bought a filly by Song out of Devon Night for 7,800gns, temporarily without an owner. Did I think Edwin would be interested?

I agreed to pop down and have a look at the filly as soon as possible. Apparently, it had been Tom's intention to buy the previous lot, also a Song filly from the Littleton Stud, but it fetched too much, about 13,500gns, I believe.

He settled instead for Song's second daughter, with an inferior bottom line, that followed on through the ring.

Examination of the filly's pedigree certainly didn't give me a hot flush. The dam, Devon Night, by Midsummer Night II, had been bought out of a Goodwood seller by George Todd for 720gns and, having won two more similar contests, retired to stud.

She was eventually sold for 1,250gns to the Littleton Stud, carrying the filly in question.

The catalogue credited the second dam, Devon Violet, with a race in Germany at four years, but failed to mention that it was a military gymkhana race and the winning rider was General "Monkey" Blacker's wife Zulu. Incidentally, both were no mean pilots whether to hounds or on a racecourse.

In view of this family history, close on £8,000 appeared to be plenty enough money to pay. However, I pushed off down to Tom's where he greeted me with a strong anaesthetic before leading me to the slaughter at Green Lodge.

I was not expecting to be bowled over by her looks as Tom had described her on the phone merely as "a pretty little tit who could give Edwin a lot of fun."

Sure enough, she fitted that description perfectly and, after a couple more glasses of bubbly I said: "Yes, she'll do the job well. I can just see her bowling down the hill at Epsom, goaded on by roars and shouts from Edwin and his entourage up in the McAlpine box."

Edwin asked me if I would break the news to his wife Mollie because she had recently given him a reprimand for having too many horses in training.

I awaited a lull in the conversation at the dinner table and then pounced. "Mollie, you're very clever at the naming game. Can you think of one for a filly by Song out of Devon Night?"

After a short pause for thought, she replied: "How about Devon Ditty?" With a wink from Edwin, who had clearly been earwigging from the far end of the table, he chipped in: "Darling, what a brilliant suggestion!"

Voila! Devon Ditty had entered the fold without lies or deception — a fairly crafty double act if I do say so myself

Mind you, I had become a dab hand at concealing the facts. At a previous gathering I'd given the total in training as nine, while failing to mention that the horsebox driver had already been alerted to take five yearlings on a round trip from Dobsons Stud via Epsom, Compton and Sheriff Hutton, a few days hence.

In early April, when having the routine Sunday morning natter with the trainers to get filled in before Edwin came on the blower, I thought Tom, who was not one to flaunt his geese as swans, was decidedly bullish about Devon Ditty.

He told me: She has done well and can run a bit. We'll give her a breeze-up at Sandown."

Devon Ditty ran a pleasing race, finishing about fifth. Paul Cook reported: "She'll improve a stone for the race and is sure to win a contest."

[134]

The next venture was at Pontefract. Tom was unable to attend, but Edwin and I set off in the chopper and were well briefed by his assistant, Alec Stewart.

Sitting up like a policeman, Jimmy Bleasdale, at that time the golden wonder boy of the North, had only to guide her to win comfortably.

As he slid down he said: "Do you realise this filly is top class?" Edwin nodded politely and, turning to me, observed wryly: "Where have we heard that one before?"

Her next venture was the Hilary Needler Trophy at Beverley, which she won with a bundle in hand.

We were beginning to think that Bleasdale might be right and Tom recommended a crack at the Queen Mary at Royal Ascot.

Greville Starkey, who had taken over as pilot, got so badly shut in that he had to accept the situation and finished third. In his opinion, he ought to have won with both hands full.

DEVON DITTY and Greville Starkey land the Cheveley Park Stakes from Kilijaro (left) and Do Be Daring (rails).

By now Tom had really got his tail up and suggested the filly should take her chance in the Cherry Hinton at Newmarket. She duly won in the style of a very high class filly.

On to the Princess Margaret Stakes at Ascot, which proved to be nothing more strenuous than a blow-out for a further step up to the Lowther Stakes at York. Again she won with Greville sitting as still as a church mouse.

The Flying Childers, a Group 1 event at Doncaster, was the next target. With Greville cocking a snook at the opposition, she won yet again. In fact, I couldn't recall having seen a race of that calibre won with more ease.

Now for the real test, the Group 1 Cheveley Park Stakes at Newmarket. But hold your horses. It looked as though the luck might be running out when Tom reported that the filly had an enlarged joint full of heat and must be considered a doubtful starter.

However, his head man Fred Flippance did a great job and got her to the races by using one of Sam Armstrong's old remedies: cabbage leaves under the bandages at exercise and standing with bandages soaked in warm Epsom salts each evening.

Greville rode a peach of a race to win cosily without letting her down as he feared she might feel the joint when off the bridle, or even break down in the attempt.

This unique little flying machine was now the winner of seven races worth over £81,500, a European record for a two-year-old, and just for good measure had netted £30,200 in breeders' premiums.

Edwin was now in a position most owners would dream about. He owned the leading two-year-old, which had made him richer by well over £100,000, and clearly he had a strong contender for the One Thousand Guineas.

However, he was an extraordinary character and I really do believe he was just as happy, possibly more so, having his monkey on a home bred plater at Epsom, especially if we had travelled to the meeting together by chopper, well laden with liquid refreshment, a variety of sandwiches, and a really good cigar.

He once said to me when a friend of his had a highly fancied contender for the Derby: "I don't envy him the anxiety one little bit. He'll have the squitters all the winter worrying whether it will train on, remain sound, or have a snotty nose on the morning of the race.

"The sort of horse I like is the one you can cut, chuck out in the field, and forget about until the following spring, concentrating meanwhile on the jumpers."

We went into winter quarters kidding ourselves that Devon Ditty would stay the mile, but after her first serious bit of work I sensed we all had our doubts.

In fact, on leaving the gallops, I phoned Edwin immediately and expressed that view to him. He said: "Never mind, perhaps we can have a good old punt on her in the Wokingham."

When I related this story to the handicapper I thought he was going to do himself a mischief!

She ran in the seven-furlong Nell Gwyn Stakes in preparation for

**DEVON DITTY . . . sharp
little filly with an unfashionable pedigree.**

the fillies' classic. Showing a lot of speed, she finished second to One In A Million and it was apparent then that she was basically a sprinter.

Even so, she ran a great race in the Guineas, being prominent until the Dip where lack of stamina told and she finished fifth, beaten about five lengths.

The filly was clearly worth a great deal of money by now and when I advised Edwin to sell I came under strong fire from those who prefer to mind other people's business rather than their own.

In my humble opinion, Devon Ditty was a freak and on her pedigree might never produce anything of much account.

As usual, Edwin, for better or for worse, accepted my advice and Robert Sangster paid a very substantial figure for her. Naturally, I would be monitoring her future with some trepidation.

Although we were pleased that she continued to run some very good races for her new owner, she failed to recapture her former brilliance.

At stud she bred three winners of not much account, but I had little reason to regret the advice I had given to Edwin.

What a fairy story - a sharp little filly with an unfashionable pedigree, bought cheaply on spec, wins a maiden at Pontefract and then graduates to the Cheveley Park at Newmarket to become the record breaking two-year-old of Europe.

Great credit to Tom Jones, his staff and to Greville Starkey, who rode her to victory so stylishly without once picking up his shillelagh.

And what happened to the dearer Song filly? She never raced at two and never won at all.

Colourful Clive's Brighton Coup

MY INVOLVEMENT with the horse world has brought me in touch with many colourful characters and recollection of Clive Graham, brings back very happy memories. He had a unique sense of humour, an uncanny knowledge of the Turf, and as a racing journalist and broadcaster will be remembered long after we have fallen off our perches.

I enjoyed his friendship immensely and never tired of his racing stories, full of skullduggery and sex, told with that warm and distinctive voice.

As a matter of routine we would meet in the bar before the first race for a glass of bubbly and exchange of information. Apart from something to punt on, he was always well briefed concerning the matrimonial entanglements of the training fraternity.

As a side line, Clive advised Desmond Molins on his racing and breeding activities and was genuinely upset to learn that their old horse Hadrian was to suffer a fate worse than death the following day.

A grand little chestnut horse, he was home-bred by Saint Crespin III out of the Ridge Wood mare Rosebag and had won and been placed in numerous top handicaps, including such races as the Victoria, Bunbury and Crocker Bulteel Cups.

Clive, while adding that he didn't know what he'd use for cash, asked me if I would train the old chap should he manage to rescue him. The thought of Clive as an owner had to be good gas.

He rang back and sounded delighted to say he'd clinched a deal for a monkey, and that Hadrian would be in my yard within the hour just in case Desmond changed his mind, something he was prone to do.

Randall Knight, an owner and a very good friend, was in the yard when the box arrived. An immensely kind and caring person, he was touched to hear the story and offered to take a half share. Clive was delighted and insisted their new acquisition should carry Randall's name and colours.

The three of us had the greatest fun planning and scheming how to manipulate an old fashioned coup. Clive knew all the horse's idiosyncrasies and in his opinion Hadrian needed seven furlongs, blinkers, bottomless ground, Tony Murray at the controls, and, like Greta Garbo, preferred to be on his own.

Being so high in the handicap, he was difficult to place. I searched the programme book for a likely target and a seven- furlong conditional seller at Brighton on June 14 stood out like a sore thumb.

At the weights he would be a knocking bet, and a full horse at eight years would hardly attract a deal of interest at the subsequent auction.

Meanwhile, Clive and Randall suggested that Kenny Bedford, the lad doing the horse, should be given a few rides in public to sweeten the old fellow, while hopefully earning him the reputation of having gone to the pack!

Well in advance of our objective, I had a word with Tony Murray to explain the plan. He agreed to ride, saying: "If he's half as good as he used to be he'd win that sort of race pulling a cart."

I planned to run another horse that day, a grey beast called Vagabond King, owned by Edwin McAlpine. Having won very easily at Leicester a fortnight previously, I thought he would go in again unless there was something which had been on the hook all season.

When the entries appeared, a Brighton double looked very possible, especially if the ground came up soft. The previous night the skies opened and it was still pissing down when we arrived at the course, engulfed by a thick sea fret and looking decidedly damp and dreary.

Randall had been appointed to handle the commissions assisted by two punter pals, who were geared to position themselves on the bottom step of the stands immediately opposite the bookmakers they had been appointed to confront.

On a pre-arranged signal from Randall, sighted at the end of the line and up a few steps, they would advance simultaneously and place their wagers. I gathered the signal was a large white handkerchief being pulled out of the gang leader's breast pocket with a flourish.

Although smacking of Nat Gould and perhaps amateurish in conception, it was fun and what's more it paid off most handsomely!

The paddock was awash and Tony Murray said: "He'll love this ground. I'll pop him out and let him bowl along, then tack across to the stands rail."

I said: "That's fine, but can he win?" Came the quick reply: "More to the point, can he swim?"

They're off. Hadrian, swinging along on the bridle and relishing the quagmire, edged across to the stands side and won comfortably all on his own under the nearside rail.

It went without saying we would buy him back whatever the price. The palm of the second trainer had been crossed, and as the auctioneer, resembling a drowned rat, was trying to get a bid from a gawping handful of onlookers, I said: "You're wasting your time. Come and have a drink."

Very wet, but very happy, the entourage headed for the bar where Randall and his pals had already set up three bottles of champers. Their operation in the ring had worked with precision and the lolly was on at 9-2.

Loving every minute of the intrigue, Randall said: "They tell me the dogs have been barking and a lot of money is expected over the blower for Vagabond King, so we plan to go in early and take first offers."

Edwin and I left the celebrations to have a word with Joe Mercer. No instructions were needed as he had ridden the grey when trained by Dick Hern and on whose advice I'd purchased the horse.

Vagabond King went to the front three furlongs from home and won nicely amid roars and shouts from his inebriated connections. Randall reported that his team had snapped up the opening price of

7-2, after which a contagious flood of money forced the odds down to 2-1 at the off.

An unforgetable day. Clive was obviously thrilled, as was his partner, already high from his punting escapade. In fact, he admitted it was the most exciting day of his life and two days later he arrived with two crates of champagne for me and a cartoon of the Brighton sensation which he had painted himself.

Hadrian went on to win a further seller at Windsor some weeks later, ridden by Pat Eddery. All concerned agreed that the old fellow had earned his retirement and he joined Edwin's stud as teaser for Birdbrook, the resident stallion.

To avoid frustration, we allowed him to screw a few old pony mares on the side, a pleasure only made possible by Clive's compassion.

One day out of the blue, Clive said to me: "Max Aitkin is giving a do in my honour at the Garrick. I would very much like you to come."

When I enquired what the party was in aid of, he smiled and said: "I imagine the bugger is going to sack me." I laughed and didn't give it another thought, but soon I realised his remark was a smokescreen.

Jocelyn Stevens, who was drawn next to me, appeared amazed that I was unaware that Clive was terminally ill with cancer. He explained that the function was to thank Clive for all he had done and to bid him farewell.

I was shattered. I just couldn't believe that this great character would shortly be leaving the racing scene for ever. The rest of the evening was unreal, although I do just remember Lord Rosebery, Max Aitkin and Peter O'Sullevan saying a few words.

Alas, about a week later, Clive's warm and croaky old voice, now somewhat slurred, came down the phone. "Mike, could you come and see me. There is something I have to do urgently and I need your help."

At Max's insistence, Clive had been transferred from the rundown St George's Hospital to the Devonshire Place Clinic.

With its tariff as high as the nearby Post Office Tower, it appeared to be the mecca for patients from the oil-rich Arab states. Hence, as Clive's personality became transformed by steroids, his regular evening visitor was his longtime friend and partner on the Daily Express, Peter O'Sullevan.

Peter told me that on one occasion they had been for a walk round the block and were making their ascent in the lift to the third floor. Surrounded by fellow passengers dressed in voluminous white robes, Clive shattered the general silence with the forcefully delivered advice: "Mind your shoes, Pedro. This place is full of camel shit!"

When I got to the clinic he looked ghastly, but in his usual flamboyant manner said: "While I get mobile help yourself to a bottle of fizz from the cupboard, old cock, then we're off to see the tobacconist around the next block."

I immediately offered to carry out the errand on his behalf, as clearly he was not fit to go anywhere. However, he was adamant and, totally out of character, became quite aggressive. "Don't be such an effing old woman. Let's get cracking."

Ignoring him, I went down the corridor to the matron's office to ask her permission. She said: "I don't envy your task, but take him by all means. It can do no harm as his time is running out fast. Should you meet any problems hail a cab and bring him back. She shouted after me: "Ignore him if he becomes offensive — that's caused by the medication."

I'm not a squeamish person, but I didn't relish the task ahead. Clive told me to take his arm and not let anyone see that he was in trouble. On the way he tried to explain why he had to go to the tobacconist personally.

It appeared that an old friend had kindly sent him a lot of his favourite cigarettes, but no more could he smoke, and a regular visitor, who he described as a kind-hearted old crook, had insisted on flogging off the fags on his behalf, boasting that he had screwed an unsuspecting shop assistant for much more than their worth.

This obviously worried Clive, who was determined to apologise and put matters right. Stumbling out of the shop, he said: "Thanks, Mike. I wouldn't have wanted to die with that on my conscience."

When eventually we got back to the room, Percy Hoskins was waiting to see Clive, and after we had finished the bottle together I bid him adieu for the last time.

You may wonder why I include such a sad sequel to an otherwise happy period of fun and friendship. I do so as a means of saluting a very brave and caring man. God bless him.

**HADRIAN (Pat Eddery, second right),
wins the Windsor seller from Apelles (Lester Piggott, second left)
and Zamberex (Duncan Keith, rails)**

**CLIVE
GRAHAM**

Drawing On An Artist's Experience

WE WERE going through a sticky patch in the summer of 1954. Three of our so-called good things had been turned over, but I had a couple more up my sleeve, which hopefully were capable of pulling us out of the mire.

Both were engaged at the two-day Whitsun meeting at Hurst Park. Loll was in a race on the Saturday and Pronto had an engagement on the Monday.

Loll had been extremely unlucky at Epsom a fortnight earlier, the pilot having ridden a most extraordinary race for which he was suspended for the remainder of the meeting.

I engaged Harry Carr to ride at Hurst Park and frankly I couldn't visualise his being beaten unless an unforeseen bogey intervened.

Harry arrived very late in the parade ring, breathless, clearly very agitated, and only just in time to throw his leg over. During the race he totally disregarded the plans we had mutually agreed earlier and duly got beaten half a length.

On dismounting he said: 'I'm very sorry, Major. I should have won, but my mind was not on the job. What will they do to the Captain? Do you think he'll lose his licence?'

Frankly, at that particular moment, I wasn't thinking what they might to to the gallant Captain. I was more concerned that we had been robbed of a decent touch and Loll deprived of two consecutive races through no fault of his own.

Even so, I must tell you of the episode that indirectly caused our latest downfall as it really was the most hilarious horserace I've ever witnessed.

Half an hour earlier in the two-mile Winston Churchill Stakes, Harry had ridden a very good stayer called Premonition, trained by Captain Cecil Boyd-Rochfort. The horse had won the St Leger the previous season and was a racing certainty at 8-1 on.

There were six runners and he had a pacemaker belonging to the same owner called Osborne, a useful horse in his own right, ridden by work rider Roy Burrows. Osborne was among the 25-1 others.

Osborne set off in front at a decent clip, as he had done the previous month in the Yorkshire Cup, which Premonition had won by four lengths.

About four furlongs out, Carr was starting to send out distress signals, kicking and scrubbing, but all to no avail, while Burrows was swinging along in front with aching arms.

With only a furlong to go, Burrows was now standing up in his irons like a cowboy, trying to pull Osborne back, but the more he tugged the better the horse went.

Meanwhile, Carr, riding like a man possessed, was gradually closing the gap and in the last 50 yards drew level as the two horses flashed past the post locked together.

All the experts were of the opinion that Burrows had been unable to anchor Osborne and had won very narrowly, but the judge, obviously an officer and a gentleman, sportingly declared Premonition as the winner by a short head.

The Captain, who trained both horses, was, of course, beyond reproach and, as the Queen's trainer, was a cut above other licence holders, the majority of whom he referred to by their surnames only.

His assistant once said that, unlike his fellow men, the Captain was of the opinion that if he broke wind the draught would smell of roses.

Although protesting vigorously, the Captain was summoned to attend an inquiry in the Jockey Club Rooms at Newmarket.

This would normally be held at Cavendish Square, but I suppose the Newmarket venue was more convenient as it allowed him to be home in time for lunch.

For the first time in history, a maximum fine of £100 was imposed. I can vouch for the authenticity of the punishment because half an hour later I suffered exactly the same sentence for an offence which bore no comparison of severity.

Referring to the inconsistency of the stewards, a humorous young racing scribe reported the next day that in his opinion Boyd-Rochfort should have been locked in the Tower for the rest of the season.

On the other hand, he wrote, Pope should have been let off with a rap over the knuckles for his misdemeanour and the stewards' secretary responsible for sneaking on him castrated forthwith.

It was now up to Pronto to get us out of trouble. He had run a very decent race at Lewes ten days earlier when in need of the outing and had subsequently done an encouraging bit of work.

I alerted my owners, Edwin and Mollie McAlpine, that I was confident we could retrieve some of our recent losses handed to those brigands, who prefer to be known as turf accountants.

Bill Rickaby was to ride and I had asked Bill Tarrant to do the commissions for us. He elected to back the horse at S P, whilst suggesting Edwin and I should have a few quid each-way in the ring on the danger, making it as obvious as possible that we were opposing our own horse.

Although immaterial as it turned out, Pronto drifted from 5-2 to 4-1 at the off.

As the runners walked round the ring our fellow looked different class, being such a fine, big, dapple grey and a very swanky walker.

I began to think it was like taking candy from a baby and told Rickaby: "Jump off and let him bowl. You'll win all right."

Pronto struck the tapes well enough but was always being niggled along and never looked like winning. Rickaby said: "Sorry, but I was never going well at any stage and can only think there is something wrong with him."

Edwin, Mollie and I were standing gazing at the horse in disbelief, trying to fathom the reason for his dismal display, when we noticed an oldish man, dressed in a tweed suit and bow-tie, with battered trilby and rolled brolly, clearly eavesdropping on our conversation.

Mollie, in a mood of despair, having lost her lolly, said: "Well, if you ask me the horse is only fit for cat's meat."

At this the inquisitive gentleman stepped forward and, doffing his hat, said: "Madam, you are talking utter nonsense. That horse is a magnificent individual: his conformation and bone structure are faultless; in fact, he is a perfect equine specimen. He is clearly off colour today, but could be as right as rain in the morning."

By now, of course, I had recognised the interloper as none other than Sir Alfred Munnings the famous equine artist and, before Mollie had a chance to lambast him with her umbrella, I stepped in to introduce them.   Soon they were getting on like bosom pals.

**CAPTAIN
SIR CECIL BOYD-ROCHFORT**

**SIR ALFRED
MUNNINGS**

689-692   Hurst Park, June 5, 1954
3671f 8 Rn   2m 8 3/5 (3 2/5 under av)
690 WINSTON CHURCHILL STKS (C & F) £2434 5s 3.30 (3.31)
                              abt 2m 70y
486* Premonition 4-9-0 WCarr 3rd st: rdn 4f out: led nr fin —1
486 Osborne 7-8-7 ..RBurrows led tl hdd by wnr: fin on bit s.h.2
594 PrinceArthur4-8-4 Smirke 5th st: chall bel dist: ev ch:
                              nt qckn fnl f 2.3
346⁴ Friseur 4-7-13 ..WSnaith 4th st: no ch fnl 3f 10.4
371 Royal Task 4-7-13 FDurr 2nd st: sn droppd bhd 10.5
     SpanishStar4-8-4 Marland !w: a.in rear 4.6
1/8 PREMONITION (op1/7), 100/8 PrinceArthur(firm).Friseur(op
10/1), 25 Ors. Tote 2/4: 2/2 7/5 (12/8). Brig W P Wyatt (Boyd-
Rochfort, N'mkt) 6 Rn   m 33 3/5 (flag)

**PREMONITION's win at Hurst Park in the Winston
Churchill Stakes recorded for posterity by Raceform.**

Mind you, the horse was a typical Munnings subject: a hard, dappled grey with great presence, silver mane and tail and a big bold eye. He was just the sort of horse portrayed on an expensive box of chocolates.

Edwin, cheerful as ever in spite of his financial setback, said: "Always look forward, never look back. When is the horse entered again?"

"Not really sure," I said. "I have a feeling he is in at Birmingham tomorrow."

"Oh, good. If he's all right in the morning let's have a bash and test the Munnings theory."

In fact, the colt licked out a big feed and when trotted out first thing was jumping, kicking and farting like a good 'un. I shouted to the lad: "Take him back in, boy. You're off to Brum after breakfast."

In those days there were no overnight declarations. You simply declared to run three-quarters of an hour before the time of the race.

On scanning the Sporting Life for a spare jockey, Manny Mercer was available but, to my horror, I noticed that the race was a seller.

Immediately, I phoned Edwin to say that on Pronto's Hurst Park running we couldn't risk having a bet in order to buy him back if he won, so we'd better scrap the idea.

He replied: "Never mind. Let's take a chance and run him. I want to test the Munnings theory."

I was far from happy because should the horse produce his true form he would win on the bridle in which event I might lose him.

With no time to carry out one of my camouflage jobs to create an enlarged tendon, joint or hock, I decided to try a trick that a bent little old trainer, long since gone, had told me was especially effective on a grey horse.

I sent for my travelling lad and told him what I wanted him to do. "Give Pronto's near-fore a real good soaking in iodine before you put his travelling bandages on. Hopefully, by the time he runs the leg will be well stained, resembling the effects of a working blister.

We'll run him in crepe bandages and, if he wins, when the auctioneer tells you to take them off I will make a big show of examining the leg in order to draw attention to the suspect tendon.

[149]

"They're off." Pronto is always handy and travelling smoothly, Manny having only to let out a reef to win easily.

On dismounting, he whispered: "Be sure to buy this fellow back, guv'nor. He's a bloody nice horse."

Now for the auction. After the bandages had been removed, I ran my hand down the "doctored" leg and the deception appeared to have worked, but just as the hammer was about to fall for the third time a rough-looking little bloke in a flat cap started to bid.

However, at 420 gns the auctioneer clearly realised that the fellow bidding was stone drunk and, ignoring him, announced: "Bought in."

**PREMONITION and Harry Carr
get home by a narrow margin at Hurst Park.**

We were delighted to have retained the horse at a figure way below his true value and a month later he returned to Birmingham to win a non-seller in good style.

I don't know if there is a moral to the Pronto saga, but I do know that if it hadn't been for Sir Alfred Munnings' interference the horse might well have found his way into a tin of Whiskas instead of providing us with a great deal of fun and sport, subsequently winning many races over hurdles and fences.

**PRONTO shows his rivals a clean pair
of heels as he takes the last flight.**

Where There's Luck There's Money

OWNING racehorses has always been a rich man's hobby. A lot of luck is also needed as you will have gathered from my earlier story about Devon Ditty, an ugly duckling of a filly, who turned out to be the leading two-year-old of her sex.

The following season, Devon Ditty's owner, Edwin McAlpine, asked me as manager to warn his trainers that he was not in the market for any yearlings, having eight of his own to go into training. In fact, I think he felt it foolhardy to press his luck.

Thankfully, as it turned out, Devon Ditty's trainer Tom Jones had already pushed off to Ireland for Goffs' sales, unaware of the message.

On arrival, he bumped into Johnnie Alexander, who implored him to go and have a look at his yearling.

A quick glance at her pedigree, by Tyrant out of the Tacitus mare Tack, didn't exactly set the adrenalin flowing.

However, out of politeness and an excuse to give the bar a miss, off he went with Johnnie and his wife Chloe.

At first they had difficulty getting a head collar on the animal as she kept screwing her tail-end round, threatening to let drive.

To best recall the episode that followed I quote Tom's own words: "She was quite the ugliest-looking cow I have ever seen — very small, with a plain coffin-like head, mean little eye and ewe neck. Her only redeeming feature was a big, powerful backside.

"Once out of the box, she planted herself and refused to budge in any direction. Obviously very embarrassed, Chloe bravely volunteered to lunge her on an open space behind the boxes.

"With assistance from all and sundry, the beast suddenly took off, dragging her handler along on the end of the rein."

It was altogether an unsatisfactory display for a potential buyer, but Tom had sussed one thing. The miserable little article could really use herself and, with such powerful quarters, might well be able to catch pigeons.

In the sales ring, she slouched round, swishing her tail and showing the whites of her eyes. There was clearly some sort of reserve as the auctioneer was plucking imaginary bids from rows of disinterested faces.

Tom found himself giving a nod and then chanced another. Bang! Down came the hammer and he was landed with her for better or worse.

On scanning the sales report the following morning, I spotted that H.Thomson Jones had bought a cheap one that might be earmarked for a certain sporting peer, who enjoys a gamble.

Lo and behold, two days later Tom was on the blower. "Mike, I've gathered up a yearling that might do your job."

When I replied that I'd pop down and have a look, he said with a giggle: "Oh hell, I'd hoped you might take her unseen as she really is the most horrible-looking object I've ever clapped eyes on."

He added: "She has one redeeming feature, a backside like an old-fashioned cook. I leave it to you how much you tell Edwin, but please do your best or else I'll be stuck with the bitch."

In fact, I told Edwin the full story, which sent him into fits of laughter. He immediately picked up the phone. "Tom, old boy, I'll take that wild beast you've got lumbered with. Sounds like she's got plenty of guts and a mind of her own. That's how I like my ladies!"

Tom was normally very good with progress reports, but on this occasion there was a deathly hush for some weeks and I feared the worst.

Eventually, under pressure, I enquired after the filly, now called Trevita. With a guffaw, Tom said: "I hoped you wouldn't ask. She has been a right cow, but such a unique character we've all become rather fond of her."

Over the coming weeks the news became increasingly less depressing. "When we do get her on the heath and she condescends to jump off, there are definite signs of ability. I suggest we bung her off to Yarmouth and see what happens," said Tom.

Paul Cook, aware of the idiosyncracies, was told to let her run her own race and get as close as he could without hitting her. As Tom put it: "If you show her the stick she'll probably turn round and bite your foot off!"

The opposition may well have been moderate, but Trevita did nothing wrong and, quickening impressively, won by five lengths with Paul doing an impression of Lester Piggott with his bum cocked in the air!

Her next race was the up-market Sweet Solera Stakes at Newmarket. In she went again, beating a useful filly called Vielle quite comfortably. After finishing fourth in the Hoover Fillies' Mile at Ascot, we gave her best for the season.

Her first objective as a three-year-old was the Fern Hill Handicap at Ascot and, in spite of having to hump 9st 6lb all the way from the Golden Gates, she won nicely but still doing her own thing with the minimum of pressure from the pilot.

In fact, he was sitting so still some smart arses thought she had come up on us!

The next venture was the New Stand Stakes at Goodwood. None of us was aware that our race was to follow the important opening of the new stand when Her Majesty the Queen unveiled a life-size bronze of a horse, so ugly it could have been Trevita herself!

It was a sweltering hot day and our filly had got herself into a frightful state, awash with sweat from head to tail. Before saddling, Tom instructed his staff to give her a total dousing with buckets of cold water.

As Trevita entered the parade ring, Edwin whispered to me: What's wrong with our filly? She's dripping."

Her appearance may have ruined any chances she had of being awarded the prize for best turned-out runner, but it certainly did not detract from her performance.

Swinging along sweetly on the bridle, Paul had only to let out a reef and pounce close home to win cosily — a most impressive performance by any standard.

Edwin's entourage flocked to greet her in the winner's enclosure while he was carted off to the presentation area. I accompanied him as, being so short-sighted, he had made many dreadful *faux pas* in the past through mistaken identity.

Almost immediately, Lord March appeared with Her Majesty. I nudged Edwin sharply. "Look up, it's the Queen." He bowed from the waist and, as the presentation was about to commence, the tannoy announced: "Stewards' inquiry".

The winner was not involved, but, of course, the ceremony had to be delayed until the all-clear.

SARAH THOMSON JONES
greets Trevita after her victory at Goodwood
on the day the new stand was officially opened.

This caused a rather embarrassing hiatus of some ten minutes, leaving the select and distinguished gathering to make polite conversation. Meanwhile, Lord March was left holding the baby, as you might say. Tom, his wife Sarah, and I stood close by awaiting to applaud the presentation. A smallish man joined us as if he was a member of the party and Sarah confronted him in rather a distrusting manner.

"Who are you and what have you got to do with the ceremony?" Looking somewhat surprised, he replied: "I am the architect who designed the new grandstand." Came the retort: "Oh, bully for you. So you're the culprit!"

To be fair to Sarah, she was by no means the only one who thought the new building was a monstrosity and totally out of keeping with the glorious Goodwood countryside.

**TREVITA wins the Fern Hill
Handicap at Ascot from Restful.**

The next race for Trevita was the Prix de Psyche, a Group race at Deauville. On arrival at this beautiful course, the first person we bumped into was Stuart Murless, who trained at The Curragh. He had a runner in our race, but we assured him he was wasting his time.

Stuart and I had been good chums since the last war when we served as troopers in the Household Cavalry. In those days, together with a number of racing folk, including Jakie Astor, jockeys Danny and Tommy Morgan, and Sean Magee, we were under orders to defend Windsor Great Park to the last man!

Our task was to patrol the area at night on our dashing black chargers, with drawn swords, to protect King George VI and his family from air attack by German paratroopers.

With no specific orders on how best to engage such a force while on horseback, sporting tin hats and gas masks, we planned to let them float down from the skies until within range and then thrust them up the never mind while chanting the war cry: "How's that for centre?"

**A royal occasion as the Queen is about to present
the winner's trophy to Lord McAlpine. Lord March holds
the trophy pending the result of a stewards' inquiry.**

Happily, or perhaps sadly, we never did have the satisfaction of testing the accuracy of our aim!

Now back to Trevita's trip to France. She ran a terrific race, being most unlucky to be beaten a head. The winner was Sovereign Dona, trained by, wait for it, none other than the gallant ex-trooper Murless.

Tom told us that George Strawbridge would be interested in buying the filly to race in the USA and his offer was much too tempting to refuse.

However, she more than justified her purchase price by becoming the leading handicap mare of the year in America.

So, once more, an ugly duckling purchased on spec for small money, had turned out to be a little goldmine. For lightning to strike twice in the same place surely had more to do with luck than money.

However, for Tom and his staff it was nothing but brilliant training and patient handling.

New 'Pots for Old Rope

A FEW days ago I phoned the Tote's marketing director Geoff Webster to ask him to refresh my memory regarding the Jackpot I'd landed a quarter of a century ago under rather unusual circumstances.

After he had kindly and promptly filled me in with the details, the saga came flooding back as if it were yesterday.

The Tote Jackpot had not been operating very long but I'd been lucky enough to win one of the first, albeit only a small one.

This clearly gave Frank Cundell the impression that I had a magic formula as he asked me if he might join me as a sleeping partner.

He insisted I do all the donkey work while he would sit back and await the cheques to flow, promising not to interfere unless he had a particular fancy worthy of tossing into the pot.

Kidding myself that I knew what I was doing, I decided to adopt two principles.

First, before taking part there must be a reasonable carry-over from a previously unwon pool. Second, at least two races on the card should include likely bankers.

The day arrived when both these conditions were apparent. At the Heath meeting on the Saturday following four days of Royal Ascot, there was a good carry-over and three, let alone two, very likely bankers.

One of these was Lady Magistrate, owned by Sir Edwin McAlpine, ridden by Ron Hutchinson, and much fancied for the Fern Hill Handicap.

Ken Cundell had told me he considered Moon Storm was past the post if the going was soft and Dick Hern thought Loveridge, with Joe Mercer in the plate, would take all the beating.

Rather like a racing spiv, I found myself tapping friends and colleagues for information and a little man known as "Mark the card" was a great help.

Mark could always be found by the entrance to the weighing room, and while his tipping wasn't all that accurate his information concerning those that were not going to win for one reason or another was spot on.

It was a ghastly day, pissing with rain and blowing a gale. On arriving at the track, heavily rugged up in waterproofs, I collected a couple of Jackpot forms on the way to the bar.

Without knowledge that one could complete a permutation form to combine all numbers selected, I laboriously wrote out each line separately, making the task unnecessarily boring and tedious.

The rain was dripping off the end of my nose and the brim of my trilby making the entry form soggy and undecipherable.

In desperation I screwed it up, saying: "Oh, bugger it, I can't cope.!"

Joyce Beeby, wife of my trainer friend George Beeby, heard me and said: "Stop whinging, Mike. Let me give you a hand."

With her help and encouragement I started again. After filling in line after line, I came to the very last and in desperation merely repeated the previous one.

I hadn't a clue how much I had invested but when handing in the form for the girl to check she said: "That's £13 invested, Major Pope. May I point out that you have entered two identical combinations when you could have had another attempt for no extra expense."

Not really knowing what the hell she was talking about, I thanked her and said politely: "So be it. They say there's one born every minute."

We were well covered in the first race which Manacle won at 8-1, trained by Jack Watts and ridden by Brian Taylor. As predicted, Dick Hern won the second with Loveridge at 5-2. Now for Lady Magistrate. She was favourite at 3-1 and won comfortably.

Three up and three to go. The fourth race would have knocked out a lot of punters as there were only three runners, and the outsider of them, Wage War, was the winner at 9-2. Things were now hotting up and becoming decidedly interesting.

Pandora Bay, ridden by Taffy Thomas and trained by Geoff Barling, won the penultimate race at 4-1. We appeared to be still in but I dared not utter until I'd checked.

The smiling lady behind the jackpot window confirmed that I had two winning lines and they were both running on to Moon Storm in the last.

Squelching through a quagmire down to the saddling boxes to ask Ken Cundell if he was still confident, a bookmaker's clerk stopped me: "My guv'nor has asked me to offer you five grand for your two tickets."

Telling him to hang on for a minute, I spoke to Ken, who said: "I did fancy mine a lot but conditions are now atrocious and anything can happen."

The rain was still thrashing down like stair rods and there were rumours that racing might be stopped. I was in such a state I really do believe an abandonment would have been a relief.

I thought to myself: "What the hell. We've come this far and I'm sure Frank would want to let it roll." Unfortunately, he was at Stratford and the decision had to be mine.

Back to the bookie's runner, I said: "Thank your man for his offer, but I'm going to stay with it."

He replied: "Do you realise you've got the thick end of twenty grand going on that bleedin' 'orse? You've got guts, if nothing else, I'll give you that."

I never could find out how they even knew we were still in the Jackpot, let alone the approximate figures involved.

Never mind, up to the trainers' stand to watch the race, trying to look unconcerned when, in fact, I was trembling at the thought of gambling a small fortune on a whim. Of course, I should have hedged at least half, if not more, but what the hell!

Moon Storm, the second favourite at 9-4 and ridden by Tony Murray, was always cantering and relishing the mud won by 15 lengths. I felt distinctly sick and couldn't even raise a cheer.

Down in the lift and straight for the bar. I heard the loudspeaker announcing something about the jackpot, but clearly water had got into the works and all I could make out was ".. .each ticket paying £10,156. 4s." Gordon Bennett! And we've got two of them!

On arriving home, full of drink and soaked to the skin, the phone was ringing. It was the boss of the Tote offering congratulations, but asking if he might enquire why I had entered two identical lines.

I assured him I had no secret formula and explained that it had come about by a mixture of ignorance and impatience. He also asked why I had not completed a permutation form rather than a straight one and when I confessed my pathetic motive he laughed and said: "It's never happened before and I very much doubt it will ever happen again."

I suspected he was quite relieved to learn that it was the work of an ignoramus and not a psychoanalyst with crystal balls.

The next Jackpot was to be at Kempton on July 6. No carry-forward and, in my opinion, there was only one banker, which was my old man's Kempton specialist Birdbrook, the grey flyer, ridden by Tony Murray. I couldn't see what could beat the old horse and, ignoring my principles, got stuck in.

Up it came again, but this time only a comparatively small kitty.

We were really on a roller and by now three of my friends and owners, Guy Smith, Randall Knight and James Murdoch, had joined the team. During the rest of the season we had a lot of fun with a couple more quite healthy pots.

The Jackpot was extremely popular with thousands of small punters in those days but for me, and I guess many others, it started to lose its magical allure when the large syndicates, investing vast sums of money, came in like bulldozers whenever there was a worth-while carry-over.

I only hope that one of these days a recipe can be found to regain its popularity.

I often thought the Jockey Club should have employed Mark as a stipendary steward, but I fear his military qualifications would have let him down as he never rose above the level of lance corporal, smoked a pipe and wore a flat cap!

```
        1298 ASCOT, Sat., June 24th (Soft) Wind: slt ½ agst (DH)
                       Official times are shown
 1365          ALBEMARLE STKS (H'cap) (3-Y.O.) £956     5f      2.0 (2.2)
                           Stalls start
   861 MANACLE  8-9 .........BTaylor (12) swtg: wnt lft s: led ins fnl f:
                                           r.o wl .....................—1
   854³ Queen of Saba 8-4 ......DSmith (6) ev ch fnl 2f: unable qckn cl
                                           hme ......................¹2.2
  1030 Early Turn  7-12 ..........Cook (10) lw: gd hdwy over 1f out: ev ch
                                           fnl f: faild qckn ..........¹2.3
   718*Privilege  7-7 ..........Barclay (1) lw: rdn all wy: nvr nr to chall 2.4
   435 Scottish Mary 7-11(¹)
                     RHutchinson (11) hmpd s: gd hdwy fnl f: r.o. ...¹2.5
  1030 Welsh Bede  7-5 .........Cullen (5) swtg: led over 2f out: wknd
                                           fnl f .....................3.6
   588 Rapparee 6-10(¹)‡7 .......Dicey (2) lw: nvr trbld ldrs .........3₄.7
   588*Growing Grey 8-7 ......SClayton (4) lw: led over 2f: wknd over 1f out 0
   854 Reprise  7-2(⁴)‡5 ......EJohnson (8) swtg ......................0
   Also ran:—
   861 Horned Moon 8-7           865 Kwela Boy 7-0(⁵)‡5 AMurray (9)
         WWilliamson (3) 1274 Quicksandy7-0(7)‡7 Mannion (7)
S.P.: 5 Privilege(op13/2). 6 GrowingGrey(tchd13/2). 8 MANACLE (op7/1).
Queen of Saba(tchd10/1). 9 ScottishMary(tchd10/1). 10 Rapparee(op8/1). 100/8
EarlyTurn(op10/1).HornedMoon(op10/1).  100/ WelshBede.  100/6 Reprise.
KwelaBoy. 33 Quicksandy. Tote 32/8: 12/- 10/6 20/-. Mr C W Engelhard
(J Watts, N'mkt) 12 Rn                       63.58 sec (.42 under av)

 1366            ERROLL STKS (2-Y.O.) £946     5f        2.35 (2.36)
                           Stalls start
   826*LOVERIDGE 9-2 .........Mercer (4) lw: led aftr 1f: drvn out ......—1
   969*Ilkley Moor 9-2 .........Piggott (2) led 1f: unable qckn ins fnl f 1.2
   449⁴ Belgrave Square 8-9 ...BTaylor (1) chngd pos over 2f out: one pce
                                           fnl f .....................3.3
   857⁴ Kirkdale  8-9 .........Breasley (5) lw: stdy hdwy fnl 2f: nvr nrr 7.4
   965 Tansy 8-1‡5 ...........AMurray (7) spd over 2f ...............5.5
  1078³ Rose of Ennis 8-6 ......JWilson (3) spd 2f ...................2.6
   963 Conflagration 8-6 ......Starkey (6) outpcd ....................7
S.P.: 5/4 IlkleyMoor(11/8—11,10). 5/2 LOVERIDGE (tchd7/2). 4 BelgraveSquare
(tchd9/2). 100/8 Kirkdale(tchd100/7). 20 Rose of Ennis,Tansy. 25 Conflagration.
Tote 16/-: 7/6 6/2 (12/4). Mr J J Astor (W Hern, West Ilsley) 7 Rn
                                        unofficial time 64.3sec (.3)

 1367    FERN HILL STKS (H'cap) (3-Y.O. F) £1332   1m (st)   3.15 (3.16)
                           Stalls start
   860² LADY MAGISTRATE 8-1     (2) stdy hdwy 2f out: led over 1f
                     RHutchinson      out: comf ..................—1
   851⁴ Freeholder 7-2‡5 ......EJohnson (4) h: gd hdwy over 1f out: r.o wl 2.2
   996³ Tickle My Palm 7-8(¹) ...DSmith (5) rapid hdwy fnl f: fin wl ....2.3
  1233² Aura  8-2 ...............GLewis (3) led over 2f: ev ch 1f out: one
                                           pce ......................s.h.4
  1157*Ma Vlast 7-9‡7 (7x)·......Dwyer (1) led over 5f out: wknd wl over
                                           1f out ...................2.5
   962 Secret Ray 8-3‡5 ......AMurray (7) no hdwy fnl 2f ............6.6
  1008 Qallbashi 6-7‡7 ......Lemon (9) prom 4f ...................0
   981*Catherine's Sister 8-10 Starkey (8) t.o .......................0
   663*Dundry Hill 8-4 ........Barclay (6) lw: t.o ...................0
S.P.: 3 LADY MAGISTRATE (7/2—11/4). 4 Aura(tchd5/1). 7 DundryHill(op8/1).
Tickle My Palm(op5/1).Freeholder(6/1—8/1). 8 Catherine'sSister(tchd9/1). 10
SecretRay(firm). 100/8 MaVlast(op10/1). 33 Qallbashi. Tote 13/2: 6/2 10/-
7/8 (60/2). Sir E McAlpine (G Smyth, Lewes) 9 Rn        1m 46 (1)

 1368           CHURCHILL STKS £1263        1m 4f        3.45 (3.46)
```

**Half way there! Three races down and the
Pope team are on their way to a bumper pay-out.**

**MANACLE sets the Jackpot ball rolling for the author
in the Albemarle Handicap at the Ascot Heath meeting in 1967.**

```
1368              CHURCHILL STKS £1263      1m 4f        3.45 (3.46)
1118 WAGE WAR 4-8-7 ......GMoore mde all: drvn fnl f: r.o ...........—1
     Wrekin Rambler 4-8-10 Breasley 3rd st: hdwy fnl f: nvr nrr .........2.2
     762² St Puckle 4-8-10 .........Cook 2nd st: ev ch 1f out: one pce ...1½.3
S.P.: 4/5 St. Puckle(op11/10), 2 WrekinRambler(op5/4), 9/2 WAGE WAR(op7/1).
Tote: 17/4 (31/10). Mr H J Joel (T Leader, N'mkt) 3 Rn      2m 45.24 (8.24)
                              346

1369          FENWOLF STKS (2-Y.O.) £988    6f        4.20 (4.27)
                        Stalls start
1253*PANDORA BAY 8-12 MThomas (2) gd hdwy 2f out: led wl ins
                                     fnl f: r.o wl ..................—1
     739² Le Conquerant 8-9 WSwinburn (7) lw: led over 4f: led ins fnl f:
                                     r.o ......................1½.2
     1186³ Dynaminx 8-6 ..........GMoore (5) led wl over 1f out: faild qckn
                                     ins fnl f ..................1½.3
1193² Noble  Boy  8-9 ........DSmith (11) gd spd 5f ...............hd.4
     Daniel  8-4  ........RHutchinson (1) gd sort: scope: bkwd: rapid
                                     hdwy fnl f: shapd wl .......hd.5
     Bavard 8-4 .............Cheshire (12) gd sort: gd hdwy fnl f: fin  wl 7.6
     Gordon House 8-4 WWilliamson (14) gd sort: neat: spd over 4f ...hd.7
     722 Chevet Lane 8-9 .........Pignott (13) outpcd .....................0
     Parados  8-4  ............Starkey (3) w'like: lt-f ...................0
     Flying Finn 8-4 .........GLewis (8) gd sort: wl grwn ................0
     Pure Fiction 8-1 ........Barclay (4) w'like: scope: bkwd: outpcd ....0
     Also ran:—                303 Zarathon 8-9 ......Breasley (9)
     720² Trumpeter 8-9 ........Cook (6) 1082³ Marciano 8-9 ......WGuest (10)
S.P.: 3 Trumpeter(op11/2) 4 PANDORA BAY (tchd9/2), 6 NobleBoy(tchd7/1),
ChevetLane(op6/1). Dynaminx(op6/1). 9 Zarathon(tchd10/1). 100/8 Daniel
(op8/1). 100/6 FlyingFinn. 20 Ors. Tote 22/2: 9/4 21/6 9/2. Maj C H Nathan
(G Barling. N'mkt) 14 Rn                           1m 20.44 (2.44)

1370    ~    HALIFAX STKS (H'cap) £918     2m       4.50 (4.51)
```

STILL on target and only one race to go.

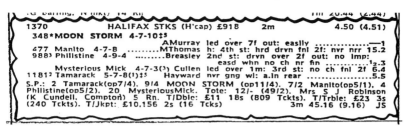

```
.G  carnng.  N hkr  14  Rn
1370            HALIFAX STKS (H'cap) £918      2m              4.50 (4.51)
348*MOON STORM 4-7-10‡5
                          AMurray led over 7f out: easily .............—1
477  Manlto  4-7-8    .........MThomas  h: 4th st: hrd drvn fnl 2f: nvr nrr 15.2
988) Phillistine  4-9-4  .........Breasley  2nd st: drvn over 2f out: no imp:
                                       easd whn no ch nr fin ...........¹2.3
       Mysterious Mick  4-7-3(³) Cullen led over 1m: 3rd st: no ch fnl 2f 6.4
1181² Tamarack  5-7-8(1)‡5   Hayward  nvr gng wl: a.ln rear ...................5.5
S.P.: 2 Tamarack(op7/4). 9/4 MOON STORM (op11/4). 7/2 Manlto(op5/1). 4
Phillistine(op5/2). 20 MysteriousMick. Tote: 12/- (49/2). Mrs S J Robinson
(K Cundell, Compton) 5 Rn. T/Dble: £11 18s (809 Tckts). T/Trble: £23 3s
(240 Tckts). T/Jkpt: £10,156 2s (16 Tcks)                3m 45.16 (9.16)  JS
```

They've done it!
Moon Storm's victory meant
drinks all around for Pope and his supporters.

FRANK CUNDELL:
partner

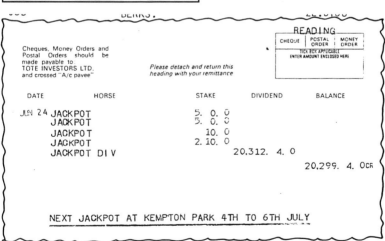

```
                    BERKS.                        22.0100

                                              READING
                                        CHEQUE | POSTAL  | MONEY
                                               | ORDER   | ORDER
  Cheques, Money Orders and                 TICK BOX APPLICABLE
  Postal  Orders  should  be              ENTER AMOUNT ENCLOSED HERE
  made payable to:
  TOTE INVESTORS LTD.          Please detach and return this
  and crossed "A/c pavee"      heading with your remittance

     DATE        HORSE          STAKE       DIVIDEND      BALANCE

  JUN 24 JACKPOT               5. 0. 0
         JACKPOT               5. 0. 0
         JACKPOT               10. 0
         JACKPOT               2. 10. 0
         JACKPOT DIV                       20,312. 4. 0

                                                   20,299. 4. OCR


     NEXT JACKPOT AT KEMPTON PARK 4TH TO 6TH JULY
```

A luvly jubbly winning
account from the Tote.

On Cloud Nine With Sky Rocket

MY OLD man had a snug and well-stocked little bar at his home across the yard from mine and many a happy hour we spent either celebrating a recent winner or plotting one for the future.

It was a well frequented watering hole, especially on Sunday mornings when visiting owners gathered to talk horse over a drink.

On the beams in the bar there were the racing plates of every winner from the yard since its creation as a training establishment.

For the first win a brass star was placed in the middle of the plate, together with the name and breeding on a small plaque. A further star was added for each subsequent success.

Around the walls hung every manner of racing paraphernalia, including enamel Members' badges, owners' browbands, and a very faded set of my old man's colours.

The latter brought back memories of a story in racing circles that credited him with being the only owner with two sets of colours. One was a highly fluorescent lime green with purple spots. The other set, although officially the same, were dull, dingy and non-luminous.

Rumour had it that the conspicuous silks were worn by the triers, while those not too busy carried the drab set. Totally false, of course.

On the eve of the horses-in-training sale at Newmarket we were having a noggin after evening stables. I had the catalogue with me as the old man had mentioned he was keen to buy another horse.

He already had four in training, but wanted to replace Birdbrook, who had retired to stud, preferably a sprinter as he was keen to have a runner in the Wokingham.

He said: 'It was a great day when you won the race with Golden Leg and I'd love to have a crack if you can find a suitable animal.'

Says I: 'Funny you should say that, I've marked off a colt called Sky Rocket, trained by Sam Armstrong and owned by the Bryces, who sold us Birdbrook. What's more, this fellow is also a grey.

'I've had a word with Sam and apparently the horse is perfectly sound, has a lot of ability, but appears to have become disenchanted with racing. If a change of scenery restores his enthusiasm he could be just the very article.'

It was agreed I should go to five grand, plus a few hundred if need be. On reaching Newmarket, I went straight down to Sam's yard.

'My eyes, what a good-looking colt, almost too good looking, in fact a bit of a pretty boy. Not too big, full of quality, a good hard grey, and limbs like bars of steel.'

The head lad said: 'If you can sweeten him up he'll win you a decent race, but at the moment he doesn't want to know about racing.'

I bought him for 3,700 gns and the old man was delighted. At this stage the Wokingham was only a pipedream but he had a lot of patience and never tried to rush me.

I decided that Billy Sargison, an exceptionally good lad who had looked after Birdbrook so well, should do the horse. We planned a long holiday for Sky Rocket to try to get him to relax and forget all about the racing game before preparing him for a few easy races without any serious questions being asked either at home or on the racecourse.

When we started to step up the tempo he clearly had two ways of going. Either he would explode and take off, or sulk and work badly. A real little bastard, as strong as a bull and when in the mood a flying machine.

My old man had a theory that a racehorse's diet was tasteless and boring. He used to stroll around the yard with a bucket full of fresh vegetables he had grown himself tempting his own horses with their individual tastes, much to the head lad's horror.

After an initial outing under Joe Mercer at Warwick, we decided to send Sky Rocket to Ally Pally for the Wheelers' Little Fish Apprentice Handicap. An unknown young Irish lad that Frenchie Nicholson had recommended was booked for the task.

The plan was to let the horse enjoy himself and do no more than he wanted to, but whilst doing just that, should he finish in the first three, there was no harm done.

In fact, he finished second to Raffingora (gave 5lb!) somewhat reluctantly, I thought. However, two or three more similar races could sweeten him for the big day.

Incidentally, that lad was to win the very first race of his career three days later at Epsom on Alvaro, a horse I had purchased on the same day as Sky Rocket. That lad's name was Patrick Eddery.

On to the Ascot Spring meeting, 11 days later, where he was third, showing a lot more enthusiasm.

A fortnight hence at Bath was to be his third sweetener with the same lad on board. This run was encouraging as, running into third place, he appeared much keener. All his races so far had been over the minimum trip but clearly an extra furlong would be in his favour.

After the race a certain universally disliked stipendiary steward approached me. 'Pope, your horse appears to have been very tenderly ridden on its last three outings. I suggest you take that observation as a friendly warning.'

I replied: 'I don't give a stuff if it's friendly or hostile and I suggest you pay heed that I intend to win the Wokingham with that horse, so stick that in the book.'

No doubt the smart arse would record my remarks so I thought it only prudent to let it be known around the corridors of power that the horse's long-term preparation had been genuinely therapeutic and in no way premeditated skulduggery.

You may think I am allergic towards stipes but then I suppose they do have to be sneaky individuals to qualify for such a task.

There are, of course, exceptions to every rule and in my time Roscoe Harvey was certainly one of them. Not only was he a very fair and helpful stipe, but a great character. However, I'm told they are all jolly decent fellows these days!

On returning from Bath, I told my old man it looked as though we were on target and that he should prepare to don his betting boots ready for the fray.

That evening two of my owners, George Clover and Louis Corazza, both close chums, phoned to say they would be away for Royal Ascot and should they leave a bet for the Wokingham? It was agreed I would put them on a hundred apiece, probably their maximum at the time.

The following day when the horse was being led out he jumped and kicked with such zest he spread a plate, two nails penetrating the sole of his foot. All the usual aids were applied immediately, but in the morning he could hardly put his foot to the ground.

A setback such as this, which entailed his being confined to his box for nearly a fortnight with an infection, would normally rule out any chance of a horse running, let alone winning. However, this fellow was so clear winded and worked best when mad fresh, we decided to let him take his chance.

Doom and gloom reigned in the yard. After nearly eight months scheming and planning, this had to happen at the most crucial stage of

**LOUIS CORAZZA (left) and George Clover -
'I think we have been duped old boy!'**

**NAIL-BITING finish
to the Wokingham as Sky Rocket
in the colours of the author's father
Alec Pope gives a young Pat Eddery
his first big win.**

Horseshoe nails nearly made Sky Rocket a damp squib

WANT of a nail cost a battle in the old story; and two nails nearly cost Sky Rocket the Wokingham yesterday.

The two nails ran into Sky Rocket's off fore when he spread a plate after a race at Bath last month.

The colt was confined to

**HEADLINE from The Life
highlighting the nail in foot story.**

the proceedings. However, the horse appeared to be in tremendous form and so mad fresh he was almost unsafe to ride out.

As regards betting, naturally our confidence had waned, so we decided to let him run free, although I believe my old man did have a few quid on to cover presents in the event of a miracle.

For preference I wanted an extreme draw, either very high or very low, so that Pat could try and make all along the running rail.

Hey presto! We were drawn four. Loaded into the stalls early, he stood like a rock until the animal in the next bay went beserk.

Creating merry hell, the banging and rattling terrified Sky Rocket, and as the traps opened he shot out like a bullet and bolted, making all down the stands rails to win at 20/1 like the most genuine horse one ever did see.

However, in Pat's opinion it was entirely due to the behaviour of the beast drawn next to him that won us the race.

Everyone was delighted and the ceremony of a star being added to Sky Rocket's plate was performed amid the popping of corks and recording of the race.

Sadly it was to be his last recognition as a racehorse because we accepted a very tempting offer for him to go abroad as a stallion.

Thank goodness I'd remembered to declare to my old chum Guy Smith before the race that I was not having a bet for our two absent friends, who, of course, were unaware of the drama which had caused their wagers to be cancelled.

When the result and starting price filtered through to Louis at Porto Santa Stefano the excitement was immense. All his friends were summoned to a Granda Fiesta when lobster thermidor was washed down with vintage champagne.

George was salmon fishing in the Outer Hebrides when he eventually received the news by carrier pigeon. He, too, released the moth from his wallet when ordering the staff at the Amhuinnsuidhe Castle to prepare a mammoth feast for his fellow anglers.

On returning home, they telephoned to say: 'Well done', without reference to the fact that they had been duped into misguided generosity. Who says that the days of noble-minded gentlemen are no more!

Huntin', Shootin'
And Puntin'

WHILE BROWSING through the Tattersalls December
Sales catalogue some 35 years ago, I spotted a batch of horses
being submitted by Major Lionel Holliday from his La
Grange Stables.

Having recently taken over as the Major's private trainer, Dick
Hern would, I felt sure, mark my card, especially as he knew full well
any derogatory information would not be leaked to the world and his
wife.

Most of the horses were fully exposed and were either at the top of
the handicap or showing some wear and tear from a long and arduous
campaign.

The Holliday horses were always trying for their lives and subjected to a rigorous training programme at home.

I phoned Dick and he said the best of the bunch would make more
than they were worth and the others were best left alone with no
questions asked.

However, there was one unknown quantity that might just be
worth a gamble, a two-year-old filly by Golden Cloud, only once raced
due to continuous sore shins.

He said she was a very gross individual with a backside like a cart mare, but a great mover with a lovely temperament. Having said that, she might, of course, be useless.

I'd been asked to shoot on the day before the sales by a good chum of mine whose old father, Brigadier Peter Gordon-Bentley, owned the Buck Hall Estate, only half an hour from the Park Paddocks.

The old man was now rationed to half a bottle of whisky per day whereas in the past he had earned the nickname of Pissy Pete due to his excessive drinking.

I phoned Tony, the son, to confirm that I would like to shoot and let slip that I'd be going to the sales the next day.

This stimulated the desired response. 'You must doss down here for the night, old boy. Quite a few of the assassins are staying over for grub, and a game of chance.'

I arrived around half past nine in the morning to be met in the driveway by Mr Snell, the head keeper.

'Master Tony has asked me to warn you that the Brigadier has gone a bit gaga. He'll be shooting today, but his loader Henderson will be at hand to ensure good behaviour.'

A big, rambling old house cluttered with priceless furniture and paintings by well known artists adorned the walls.

It had an enormous entrance hall out of which swept a vast staircase, leading to a galleried landing. We were downing a sloe gin in the hallway while Tony fiddled the draw to favour irregular guests.

'You're well placed, Mike. In fact, you're in the hot seat at the big drive, but you may suffer a bit of poaching from my old man, who will be on your right.'

'He's safe enough but a bit greedy these days. However, I've told his man to stuff only one up the spout in case he gets carried away.'

Sure enough, the first bird of the drive, a nice high cock, was coming straight to me. A shout from the Brigadier: 'Your bird, Major.'

I was nicely on and about to squeeze when 'Bang' and out of the sky the bird dropped stone dead at my feet.

Yells from the Brigadier to his decrepit old spaniel and stone deaf labrador: 'Good dogs, hi lost, hi in ther.'

**MICHAEL POPE takes a
high bird at the Long Belt Stand
without the assistance of his pistol-packin' host.**

The spaniel arrives at my peg dragging a long chain attached to a shooting stick while the labrador, so fat it could hardly walk, sniffs my leg and cocks his!

On the next drive amid the noise of the approaching beaters there was a grunting noise like the sound of a pig. Sure enough, an old sow comes crashing out of the wood and, to my amazement, Pissy Pete ups with his gun and lets go. The poor unfortunate brute, squealing like fury, crashes back into the covert goaded on by shouts of 'Tally ho' from all and sundry.

Tony had seen what was going on and, tempting his old man with a tumbler of haig, bundled him into his Land Rover with his loader and sent him packing.

The rest of the day was a great gas and at the Long Belt, the main drive of the day, the quality of the birds had to be seen to be believed.

That evening we had an excellent and most amusing dinner, recalling the events of the day, while poor old Pissy Pete had been given a tranquiliser in his Horlicks and was hopefully sound asleep dreaming of hunting boar in Hungary.

Tony and I were the last to hit the hay and on our way up the stairs I enquired as to the origin of an enormous painting covering half the wall.

'It's said to be of Diana and Acteon by Titian and insured for a vast sum, but there is some doubt as to its authenticity.'

In the early hours, I was awakened by someone pounding along the landing bawling: 'Who goes there? Stop thief or I'll fire.'

While I was leaping out of bed two resounding shots rang out. As I reached the door there was the Brigadier shouting: 'I've got the blackguard. Take him to the guard room.'

By now Tony and Henderson were grappling the gun away from the old chap and when the lights were switched on, lo and behold, there were two gaping, great holes in the painting as big as yer head. Acteon had lost his wedding tackle and Diana's tits would never no more be a pair!

After an early breakfast I set off for the sales and to cut a long story short Golden Leg was knocked down to me for 560 gns.

Naturally, I was delighted and immediately decided to keep her for myself as she would only have to win a moderate contest at Bogside to be worth ten times her purchase price as a broodmare.

But, as usual, Edwin McAlpine's secretary, Mrs Thomas, had been through the sales returns on his behalf with a tooth comb, and when I went to Tattersalls office to request that the filly be billed to me personally I was informed that they had received a telegram which read: 'Charge Golden Leg to my account. Signed Edwin McAlpine.'

On returning home, I warned him that she might be a pig in a poke and could be useless, but he said: 'When I saw which yard she had come from I thought: aye, aye, Mike's had his card marked by this old mucker, that'll do me!'

In early Spring when I started to send her along she appeared to be either bone idle or not worth tossing a coin.

However, those who had ridden her work assured me it was the former. When Greville Starkey next came down to ride work I decided to don the blinds and learn the truth.

For trial tackle I had Floss Silk, a very useful sprinter who had won three races the previous season as a two-year-old, and a speedy filly called Ablaze, who had also won the season before, and again at Leicester only 16 days before the pending gallop.

The pilots were instructed to come a real good clip and push them out with hands and heels. I told Greville that I wanted to know if he considered Golden Leg was worth persevering with. Always nicely on the bridle, she finished upsides Floss Silk, with Ablaze three lengths off. All concerned were clearly impressed and in order to dampen their enthusiasm I said in a loud voice: 'Yes, she'll win a race on that form, but I'll need to give her a couple of runs to get her handicapped.'

On the Friday of the Whitbread meeting at Sandown she was in a five-furlong handicap for three-year-olds. It looked tailor-made for the job. She had 7st 13lbs.

I told Edwin that she would take all the beating and suggested we should keep well clear of the ring and get Loll Clancy to back her late on.

In the paddock I said to Greville: 'How will she go?'

The reply came: 'Well, how would you fancy Floss Silk in this contest or even Ablaze for that matter?'

His assessment proved correct. Golden Leg was always travelling sweetly and won nicely. Loll arrived with a broad grin on his face. 'You've got 20/1 to your money.'

To show how true that trial gallop had been, Floss Silk made all to win at Newbury shortly afterwards and Golden Leg went on to win a competitive handicap at the same venue.

The following season our main objective was the Wokingham Handicap at Royal Ascot. As she was a gross mare we gave her a run at Kempton and she was a very satisfactory third.

A trip to Hamilton followed. She looked likely to win whether wanted or not and likely to start odds-on.

However, she ran well below expectations, due in the opinion of the pilot to the downhill track. We'd backed her at SP for a lot of money before leaving home, subject to even money or better. Unfortunately, she started at 11/10 against and we caught a nasty cold.

A week later we ran at Newbury, where she fooled us by winning quite cosily and carried a 12lb penalty when a good third at Birmingham a fortnight later.

In spite of this she was allotted only 7st 5lb in the Wokingham.

Tom Masson's star apprentice Bobby Elliott had been booked for some time and, with his 5lb allowance, our chances looked rosier by the minute.

All we needed was a firm surface which she relished, and preferably a high draw as she was inclined to hang to the right and liked to run along the fence. Hallelujah! Drawn 26 and officially hard ground.

On arriving at Ascot, I had a chat with the man on the gate, a jolly fellow who sold Mid-day Star and Standards, to tell him he was on to a fiver with me at the best odds available. A number of trainers and jockeys used to tell him the time of day and I found this information a useful guide when weighing up a contest.

When I booked Eph Smith for a ride the next day, he told me a story I shall never forget.

Said he: 'I hope you don't give me instructions like I had last Friday. I was told to cover him up until a furlong from home, then pull him wide and start farting right to the line.

'I thought the fellow must be as nutty as a fruitcake. How could anyone fart for a furlong with safety? So when it became dangerous to break wind any more I blew raspberries and the horse just held on.

'I shall expect a decent present and what's more they'll be getting my laundry bill! Instructions like that could cause a nasty accident!'

Now for the big jamboree. Golden Leg, always travelling well down the far rail, ran on gutfully to win an exciting race at 33/1.

Edwin must have invited half the racecourse to join in the celebrations judging by the amount of cash I had to borrow from Dickie Gaskell to meet our obligations to Flo in the bar and Harry on the gate.

When the dust had settled we decided to conclude her career with a cut at the Sunset Handicap at Manchester and Great St Wilfrid Handicap at Ripon. She won both and poetic justice prevailed. Greville Starkey and Bobby Elliott notched up one each.

Happy memories of those golden days long ago when racing was all such fun and frolic.

**GOLDEN LEG (far side) gives
Bobby Elliott a 33-1 win in the Wokingham.**

Sex
Or Soup

WITH the last war finally over my regiment was billeted in and around the Grande Hotel at Rimini in Italy. We had a small but select team of horses stabled nearby which we trained on the beaches and raced mainly at Ravenna.

The racecourse had suffered very badly from shelling but was restored to its former glory by Dick Hern, my brother Barry and a large team of German prisoners.

At the time I had a batman called Tom Rogers and whenever his name cropped up there was a cry of 'and so does his sister'. As it turned out he was appropriately named, although his parents weren't to know when they dabbed him with Holy Water that he would grow into a randy little runt with an insatiable appetite for sex.

Females succummed to his charm, the attraction of which can only have been the magnitude of his courting tackle, as neither his face nor his torso were of any great account. In fact, so puny his mates nicknamed him wanker.

Forever boasting of his assignations and sneaking a crafty glimpse at my sketches on sexual variations, a booklet which, although I say so myself, was an original work of art edited and illustrated in glorious technicolour by yours truly, however we'll come back to that later should you remain intrigued.

As adjutant I selected my own quarters, a big bedroom with a private bathroom to which I selfishly retained the key. The bath was an enormous old fashioned monstrosity fit for a sheep dip with the hot and cold water emerging into one large opening.

Sorry to bore you with the details of the plumbing but they have an important bearing on the saga that follows.

Tom came to me one morning to ask a favour. 'Sir, may I please use your bathroom this evening?' I snapped at him: 'Whatever for, you've got your own ablutions so why not use them?' He stammered: 'I have always fancied a bird in the bath and I reckon yours is just right for the job.'

Throwing him the keys, I said: 'What you do in your own time doesn't concern me. By the way, is she that attractive young Italian bird with the long, brown legs I've seen you drooling over?' With a grin he replied: 'That's her, she's called Maria and Mamma is not a bad sort either.' Odds on he'd scored with them both!

Arriving back late from Ravenna after checking arrangements and walking the course prior to racing the next day, I went straight to bed as we had an early start with five runners to make ready and box up.

Dick Hern was riding Birdcatcher and Victoria, Barry was on Pitterpat and I was to bump around on Farina and Red Sails. We usually shared the rides between us unless one was due for an easy race then a certain Corporal, who was an excellent stopping jockey, would pick up a spare.

On reaching my bedroom I could hear a hell of a shindy coming from the bathroom. 'What's up?, I shouted. The reply came: 'Your batman has had a nasty accident, the poor bugger has got his toe stuck up the tap.'

On entering, a pathetic sight presented itself. There was this poor wretched fellow lying stark naked on his back with his big toe firmly wedged. He'd drained the water to avoid freezing to death in spite of which he was limp and smothered in goose pimples. Not a pretty sight!

I suggested he should be covered with towels to warm him up whilst concealing his embarrassment. Eventually he was freed by a plumber and when asked how it happened he merely stuttered: 'I slipped on the bleedin' soap.'

In the morning he hobbled in with a mug of Liptons. His toe was bound up and sticking out through a hole in an old carpet slipper. Before I could utter a word he said: 'I'm sorry for all the trouble I caused Sir, but I went for a bit more leverage, slipped and my toe shot straight up the tap.

'Maria disentagled herself, scrambled out of the bath and scarpered. Then I yelled for help.'

Replying that I was sorry, did it hurt and shouldn't he see the M.O., he said: 'Thank you Sir for being so considerate. If you ever let me use your bath again I shall not attempt to repeat that position.'

Intrigued, I was tempted to ask for details, but surely it would be infra dig for an adjutant to discuss such sordid matters with his servant.

Normally Tom would have accompanied me to the races to look after my kit but I told him to stay back and get the ladies to massage his toe. Still laughing at the poor devil's misfortune we boxed up and set off for Ravenna.

We had a great day: Dick won on Victoria, Barry on Pitterpat, and Farina (without much help from me) just pipped Dick on Birdcatcher. Finally Red Sails completed a double for me and the fourth winner of the day for the North Irish Horse Stable.

As I may have whetted your appetite earlier with the mention of my booklet I think it only fair I should tell you how it originated.

Away back in May 1944 whilst harbouring with our tanks near Pontecorvo, awaiting a call back into the fray, the 'horsey' officers used to congregate in the evenings over a few jars when the conversation seldom strayed far from racing, hunting or sex.

My squadron leader, a very decent fellow called Gordon Russell who aped Adolph Menjou and was affectionately nicknamed the Cuban Head, had horses in training with Bay Powell at Baydon in Wiltshire and loved to have a tilt at the ring.

Being a great ladies' man he was ever keen to discuss the fairer sex. On one such occasion he said: 'I wonder how many sexual positions there really are?'

I waited for the others to air their views, which varied between eight and eighteen before putting my oar in with fifty-two! Mind, I'd had my card marked by an expert, none other than Madame at the Sphinx in Algiers who had assured me there was one for each week of the year.

Gordon, disbelievingly, retorted: 'Don't be such a prat, you're thinking of Heinz soup.' I assured him that I was not, how could one confuse sex with soup? He snapped back: 'I'll bet you a pony there aren't that many. But how can we prove it?' 'Make it fifty quid,' I said, 'and I'll draw them for you.'

Over the next few weeks I sketched a variety of positions with the help of soldiers, still conscious of sex in spite of being dosed with bromide.

They enjoyed the exercise as it made a therapeutic change from the boring ritual of lectures on current affairs. Tom also produced the odd contribution, however one would have to be a contortionist or gymnast to perform such bizarre positions!

I eventually managed to produce a small book portraying fifty-two positions tastefully displayed in coloured crayon. It really was a classic and I couldn't wait to see the colour of Gordon's money. Stalling until the full team of donkey wallopers were present I announced: 'Voila, there's your proof Gordon. You owe me fifty smackers.'

Grabbing the book he thumbed through the pages roaring with laughter in disbelief at what he saw, but suddenly he said: 'The bet is off, you've cheated by using the same position three times. The first is acceptable, the second is a replica of the first except that the bloke has kept his cap on, and in the third he hasn't removed his boots.'

I had to admit that I was fairly desperate to find the final two and agreed to come up with a couple more. Alas there was no time. With precious little warning we were ordered to proceed to the Hitler line. However, I made time to threaten Tom with a fate worse than death if he lost my booklet.

The attack turned out to be a ghastly nightmare as the first few hundred yards of the advance was through dense woodland with

**MICHAEL POPE and
Dick Hern pictured jumping the last.**

visibility down to a few yards, caused by a mixture of early morning mist and dust from enemy shells lingering in the trees.

Also, in the trees were isolated snipers strapped to the branches taking pot-shots at tank commanders who had their heads out of the turrets trying to define where they were going.

Having spotted the flash of the snipers' rifles, we soon made sure they wouldn't fart in church anymore, but sadly not before one of our troop leaders was killed instantly by a bullet straight through the head.

We eventually groped our way out of the wood onto open land when suddenly all hell was let loose. Gordon's tank was blown up with such force that he and his crew just had to be dead.

Almost before the dust had settled my tank was hit, but neither my crew nor I suffered any lasting damage. The gist of a remark made on more than one previous occasion applied yet again. 'Lucky old Pope, born with a golden horseshoe up his backside.'

Sadly, others were not so lucky that morning and we lost seventy officers and men killed or severely wounded. I hasten to add that miraculously Gordon survived, suffering terrible head wounds leaving his life in the balance for many months. A battle which was recorded as a glorious victory but in reality a catastrophic bloodbath one would give anything to forget.

We are now back where my story began in Rimini but sadly the finale was not without drama. Whilst preparing for the journey home to Blighty the tin box in which my booklet was locked went missing without trace, and just as a Brylcream boy had offered to wing it home for me.

I was shattered by its loss and can only hope the lousy thief experimented with some of the more complicated positions causing extreme pain plus a double hernia!

Thanks, however, to a very generous and supportive old man, I achieved my ambition, and am thankful to say the horseshoe implant has remained intact ever since.

Footnote: I arranged to meet Gordon at Newbury races when he was fully recovered. Holding out his hand he said: 'By the way, this is for you old cock.' On opening the envelope out fell ten neatly folded white fivers.